My Heart Sings

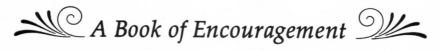 *A Book of Encouragement*

My Heart Sings

Joan Winmill Brown

WORD BOOKS
PUBLISHER
WACO, TEXAS

A DIVISION OF
WORD, INCORPORATED

MY HEART SINGS: A BOOK OF ENCOURAGEMENT

Library of Congress Cataloging in Publication Data:

Brown, Joan Winmill.
My Heart Sings.

1. Consolation. I. Title.
BV4905.2.B72 1987   242   87–18881
ISBN 0–8499–0620–2

~~ Contents ~~

⚞ *Introduction* ⚟

God is the presence, warm, all-enfolding,
　touching the drab world into brilliance, lifting
the sad heart into song, indescribable, beyond understanding,
　yet by a bird's note, a chord of music, a light
　at sunset, a sudden movement of rapt insight,
　　a touch of love,
making the whole universe a safe home for the soul.

An Early Christian

How each one of us needs a "safe home for the soul"! A place where we can find comfort and strength, where everyday problems and earth-shattering news cannot destroy our peace of mind and heart.

It has always been incredible to me that when a tornado is spawned, a fragile airplane can fly into the "eye" of the violent storm and stay long enough to measure its intensity and course. Then that same airplane can emerge untouched, unscathed by the fury that has surrounded it.

In the fury of our world, filled with the stridency of day-to-day problems and shattering world news, it is comforting to know that we, too, can find a place of calm. For even when our surroundings seem darkest, our hearts can continue to sing.

Each one of us needs a refuge—not one in which we turn our backs on the needs surrounding us, but one in which we can be fortified and encouraged so that we, in turn, may be able to help others. Our refuge is in the hollow of God's hand, surrounded by His love, and in the power that triumphed and blazed forth at Jesus Christ's Resurrection. That same power can continue to flow through all those who have received our Lord. It is a power that can make each heart sing with hope, love, and peace.

Whatever we have to experience, God faces it with us. Even when we find it hard to pray, He feels our hurts and understands our needs.

Over the years, from many inspiring writers, I have gathered together excerpts that have helped me find that "safe home." Their comforting thoughts have strengthened me, and have helped me to grow in my faith. Their reminders of God's unchanging love have so often brought peace to my anxious heart. They have taught my heart how to sing. With great joy, I share them with you.

I would like to thank Ernie Owen, Dick Baltzell, Al Bryant, and Anne Christian Buchanan of Word for making this anthology possible. Their encouragement is deeply appreciated.

May this anthology strengthen you—reassuring, supporting, nurturing a confidence within you that can make your heart sing. It may be a muted, gentle melody of God's reassurance in the midst of some dark moment—but one, nevertheless, filled with hope. Or it may be like a great triumphant hymn of praise that fills your world with joy.

Whatever your song, may it glorify our Lord, and may it reach out to a world that needs the encouragement of God's undeniable, unchanging love.

JOAN WINMILL BROWN

Part One

Touched by His Love

1

In the quiet of our hearts, we respond to His love. Our personal world is transformed —forever.

I have loved thee
   with an everlasting love:
therefore with loving-kindness
   I have drawn thee.

Jeremiah 31:3

BROKEN ALABASTER AND A MENDED HEART

The woman seemed aware of no one but the Master. That afternoon she had been among the crowd when He spoke of the *rest* He offered. His voice and His words still rang through her heavy heart:

"Come to Me, all you who labor and are heavily burdened and I will rest you. Take my yoke on you and learn of Me, for I am gentle and humble of heart, and you will find rest for your souls."

Twice she had lost Him in the crowds on the way back to the city. Then she found someone who knew He was having dinner at Simon's house. That was enough! The prejudice against public conversation with women might not have existed for her, as she ran through the darkening streets hunting Jesus.

Now she stood near enough to touch Him! She could not speak. There would have been no words. He had said He would give her *rest* if she came to Him, and somehow she was depending fully upon His understanding of her weariness. He had said she could learn about Him. That if she learned about Him, she would understand the Father! He had said He was gentle and humble of heart.

The broken, disillusioned, sinful woman stood at His feet weeping—unaware of the gaping men around the table—depending on Jesus to know of her weariness, and the burden of her wretched life.

The disciples watched their Master, confident that He would know just what to do. Simon and the other Pharisees watched Him too—watched her and watched Him. Perhaps the wretched woman had given them the opening they wanted, to trap Him. How would He handle this awkward situation? What would He do?

Jesus did nothing. He knew she was passing through the shattering moment of seeing herself as she was—in His presence! He could not spare her the shame and guilt of that moment, but *in it* with faith like hers, He could begin to heal her heart!

The woman dropped to her knees and covered His feet with her tears! Still there was no sound in the crowded room but the sound of her weeping—agonized, tight-throated sobs at first. Then with her tears still bathing His feet, the weeping grew quiet. Quiet and grateful. Quiet and grateful and relieved. Aware of a new kind of love.

Eugenia Price
(from *Beloved World*:
The Story of God and People)

CHRIST CAN GIVE THEE HEART

But Christ can give thee heart who loveth thee:
Can set thee in the eternal ecstasy
Of his great jubilee:
Can give thee dancing heart and shining face,
And lips filled full of grace,
And pleasures of the rivers and the sea.
Who knocketh at his door
He welcomes evermore:
Kneel down before
That ever-open door
(The time is short) and smite
Thy breast, and pray with all thy might.

Christina G. Rossetti
1830–1894

LOVE'S MOTIVE

Jesus never asked His men to do anything for which He did not also supply the power. What He called for, He helped to create. When He laid down the royal law of love, He supplied along with it the necessary dynamic. . . .

Jesus created love *by revealing the essential dignity and lovableness of men.* It is easy to notice a man's shabby coat, his

15

defects in grammar, his peculiar ways: Jesus went deeper, and showed that every soul was a potential son of a King. Of a scorned, renegade tax-gatherer He said, "He also is a son of Abraham" (Luke xix.9). A woman whom all good people ostracised He treated with a dignity and courtesy that might have been given to a queen (Luke vii.37). And when He said, "Take heed that ye despise not one of these little ones" (Matt. xviii.10), He was thinking, not only of the children, but of all the weak, defenceless, sensitive things of life. It does most mightily inspire love towards your fellow-men when you can see, as Jesus saw, upon every face that passes you in the street something of the image of God.

Jesus created love *by dying for men.* Every day of His life the disciples saw their Master squandering His strength for the sick and the sinful, and when Calvary came they knew that it was for sheer love of them that He had died. Can you continue to be unloving to any man, even the most unlovable, when you remind yourself—"It was for that man Jesus died"?

James S. Stewart

He that hath my commandments, and keepeth them, he it is that loveth me: and he that loveth me shall be loved of my Father, and I will love him.

John 14:21

He loves you with more than the love of friendship. He loves you the way a bridegroom loves his bride, and nothing but total surrender will satisfy Him. He has given you all of Himself, and He asks for all of you in return. For you to hold back anything will grieve him to the heart. For your sake He poured out all He had, and for His sake you must do the same.

Be generous in your surrender! Meet His measureless

devotion for you with a measureless devotion to Him. Be glad and eager to hand over the control of your life to Him. Whatever there is of you, let Him have it all. Give up forever everything that separates you from Him. From this time on, give up even your freedom of choice.

Haven't you sometimes longed to lavish your love on someone who was hardly aware of your existence? Haven't you felt such a desire for self-surrender and devotion that it seemed to burn like a fire within you, because there was no person to whom you dared give it? If so, why do you shrink back when you hear Jesus calling you into a place of nearness to Him— nearness which will require separation from everything else and will make this sort of devotion not only possible but necessary?

Hannah Whitall Smith
(paraphrased by Catherine Jackson)

Thine are goodness, grace, love, kindness, O thou Lover of men! Gentleness, tenderness, forbearance, long-suffering, manifold mercies, great mercies, abundant tender compassions. Glory be to thee, O Lord.

Lancelot Andrewes
sixteenth century

WHAT IS GOD LIKE?

The promises of God's love and forgiveness are as real, as sure, as positive as human words can make them. But like describing the ocean, its total beauty cannot be understood until it is actually seen. It is the same with God's love. Until you actually accept it, until you actually experience it, until you actually possess true peace with God, no one can describe its wonders to you.

It is not something that you do with your mind. Your finite

mind is not capable of dealing with anything as great as the love of God. Your mind might have difficulty explaining how a black cow can eat green grass and give white milk—but you drink the milk and are nourished by it. Your mind can't reason through all the intricate processes that take place when you plant a small flat seed that produces a huge vine bearing luscious red and green watermelons—but you eat them and enjoy them! You can't understand radio, but you listen. Your mind can't explain the electricity that may be creating the light by which you are reading at this very moment—but you know that it's there and that it is making it possible for you to read!

You have to receive God by faith—by faith in His Son, the Lord Jesus Christ. And when that happens, there isn't any room for doubt. You don't have to question whether or not God is in your heart, you can know it.

Whenever anyone asks me how I can be so certain about who and what God really is, I am reminded of the story of the little boy who was out flying a kite. It was a fine day for kite flying, the wind was brisk and large billowy clouds were blowing across the sky. The kite went up and up until it was entirely hidden by the clouds.

"What are you doing?" a man asked the little boy.

"I'm flying a kite," he replied.

"Flying a kite, are you?" the man said. "How can you be sure? You can't see your kite."

"No," said the boy, "I can't see it, but every little while I feel a tug, so I know for sure that it's there!"

Don't take anyone else's word for God. Find Him for yourself, and then you too will know by the wonderful, warm tug on your heartstrings that He is there *for sure.*

Billy Graham

FROM "SAUL"

'Tis the weakness in strength, that I cry for! my flesh, that I seek

In the Godhead! I seek and I find it. O Saul, it shall be
A Face like my face that receives thee; a Man like to me,
Thou shalt love and be loved by, forever: a Hand like this
    hand
Shall throw open the gates of new life to thee! See the Christ
    stand!

Robert Browning
1812–1889

LOVE

The revelation of God is Jesus Christ. 'In this was manifested the love of God toward us, because that God sent his only begotten Son into the world, that we might live through him' (I John 4:9). God's revelation in Jesus Christ, God's revelation of His love, precedes all our love towards Him. Love has its origin not in us but in God. Love is not an attitude of men but an attitude of God. 'Herein is love, not that we love God, but that he loved us, and sent his Son to be the propitiation for our sins' (I John 4:10). Only in Jesus Christ do we know what love is, namely in His deed for us. 'Hereby perceive we the love of God, because he laid down his life for us' (I John 3:16). And even here there is given no general definition of love, in the sense, for example, of its being the laying down of one's life for the lives of others. What is here called love is not this general principle but the utterly unique event of the laying down of the life of Jesus Christ for us. Love is inseparably bound up with the name of Jesus Christ for us. Love is inseparably bound up with the name of Jesus Christ as the revelation of God. The New Testament answers the question 'What is love?' quite unambiguously by pointing solely and entirely to Jesus Christ. He is the only definition of love. But again it would be a complete misunderstanding if we were to derive a general definition of love from our view of Jesus Christ and of His deed and His suffering. Love is not what He *does* and what He *suffers*, but it is what *He* does and what *He* suffers. Love is always He himself. Love is

19

always God Himself. Love is always the revelation of God in Jesus Christ.

Dietrich Bonhoeffer

. ."What manner of a man is this? I asked myself, amazed. Why does He speak with such authority, like one who brings a message from a great King? Why did the people regard Him with such joy and love, and silence fill them so that they would not miss a word? Why do they follow Him like a retinue, and crowd about Him to look upon His face and touch His garments? The children in their mothers' arms laughed with pleasure, and He smiled upon them and His face was like the sun itself. Yet what in His appearance could stir one? He wore the garments of a Galilean peasant, with poor sandals of rope, and He had no money, no servants, and He walked on foot.

"This is a quiet place, Lucanus, but from the hour when He appeared here it took on this peace you observe, this deep and holy peace, and it has never departed.

"One day, my friend, I stood at the edge of the crowd, listening, and He told the people of a prayer they must say. 'Father, hallowed be Your Name. Your Kingdom come! Give us this day our daily bread and forgive us our sins, for we also forgive who is indebted to us. And lead us not into temptation.' His voice rang over the mountains like summer thunder, and the people prayed with Him. And when they had completed their prayer His eyes suddenly found me, wondering and confused, and He smiled upon me over the people's heads. From that moment I was His, and I would have died for Him with joy. But I cannot explain why, for I am a Roman, and He was only a Galilean Jew, and a carpenter.

"Nor did this miracle come to me alone. Several of my men listened to Him also, and He took their hearts in His hand."

Aulus sighed. "I was transformed. The world of Rome was not important to me. My anxieties and troubles vanished. I was at peace. I was filled with exultation. The earth was no longer populated with enemies, but with friends. I had only one desire: to perfect myself so that I would be worthy to lie at His feet and look upon Him forever. How can one explain this? One has to experience it for himself. But I can say this: I now see all things shedding a light of their own; the moon never beamed so silvery a light before, nor was ever the sun so radiant to my eyes. Men, to me, no longer have a station; one should not be honored for mere position or wealth, but only for virtue. Moreover, all men to me now are my brothers, even the lowliest. Sometimes I say to myself, But you are a Roman, the master of the world! And it means nothing to me. Again I remind myself, We have the leadership of all the earth, and a voice in my spirit answers, That nation which seeks leadership of the earth is doomed to death, for it is an evil nation, no matter its lofty pretensions; men seek leadership only to dominate and enslave all others."

They looked upon the scene about them. The light had changed. The coiling mountains were washed with deep purple of various hues. The Sea had taken upon itself the color of an aquamarine, streaked with cobalt, and the sky was like blue enamel. Lucanus felt from it all a spiritual emanation, profound and vast and unchanging, as if unseen celestial beings hovered over all things, winged with the sun.

"One day," said Aulus, in a low voice, "they brought ten lepers to Him, weeping women and men and children. They cried to Him for mercy, and the people moved away from them in fear. But He touched them and lifted His hands over them, and they were cured instantly, and the great crowd rejoiced, and the former afflicted fell at His feet and kissed them. I saw this with my own eyes! You must believe me."

"I believe you," said Lucanus, gently.

Taylor Caldwell
(from *Dear and Glorious Physician*)

STRONG SON OF GOD

Strong son of God, immortal Love,
　　Whom we, that have not seen thy face,
　　By faith, and faith alone, embrace,
Believing where we cannot prove;

Thine are these orbs of light and shade;
　　Thou madest Life in man and brute;

21

Thou madest Death; and lo, thy foot
Is on the skull which thou has made.

Thou wilt not leave us in the dust:
Thou madest man, he knows not why,
He thinks he was not made to die;
And thou hast made him: thou art just.

Thou seemest human and divine,
The highest, holiest manhood, thou.
Our wills are ours, we know not how;
Our wills are ours, to make them thine.

Alfred, Lord Tennyson
1809–1892
(from *In Memoriam A.H.H.*)

He has an especial tenderness of love towards thee for that thou art in the dark and hast no light, and His heart is glad when thou dost arise and say, "I will go to my Father." For He sees thee through all the gloom through which thou canst not see Him. Say to Him, "My God, I am very dull and low and hard; but Thou art wise and high and tender, and Thou art my God. I am Thy child. Forsake me not." Then fold the arms of thy faith, and wait in quietness until light goes up in the darkness. Fold the arms of thy Faith, I say, but not of thy Action: bethink thee of something that thou oughtest to do, and go and do it, if it be but the sweeping of a room, or the preparing of a meal, or a visit to a friend; heed not thy feelings: do thy work.

G. Macdonald

WE'RE LOVED

It isn't easy—this business called living. But look what we've got to go on!

To have His promises is to have the pleasures of God: "Blessed be the LORD who has given rest to his people . . . not one word has failed of all his good promises . . ." (1 Kings 8:56).

That's not wishful thinking; that's truth. And because it is true, every promise yet to be completed stands with the same certainty of being fulfilled.

So we can rest, just as His people have always been able to rest, in what He has promised and what He has already given.

And from rest in Him comes the worship that says with deep feeling: "Blessed be the Lord who has given rest to his people."

From His Word come the promises; from the promises comes the resting; and in the rest are the "blesseds"—the worship.

So much is here in His Word. He didn't just give a few promises scattered now and then among demands or given occasionally to keep us going like rewards or bribes. They are everywhere, an outpouring of Himself—giving, giving, and more giving. We're loved!

We can say in worship, "Blessed be the Lord."

And out of a life lived in Him, overwhelmed by His giving, anyone can join that happy crowd spontaneously singing, "Blessed be the Lord."

It can happen. God invites it.

Don't miss the singing, because you've missed the rest. And don't miss the rest, because you've missed the promises.

Nobody has to.

Roger Palms

How incomprehensible is the love of God! His ways are indeed past finding out. How many of His providences are like the cloud between the Israelites and the Egyptians—if looked on by unbelievers, or without faith, it is a cloud of darkness; but if viewed according to the privilege of the Lord's people, it is no longer darkness, but light and safety. May this be your experience; may you feel that the Hand which inflicts the wound supplies the balm, and that He who has emptied your heart has filled the void with Himself.

Hudson Taylor

FROM A CHRISTMAS SERMON

God made Sun and moon to distinguish seasons, and day and night; and we cannot have the fruits of the earth but in their seasons. But God hath made no decree to distinguish the seasons of His mercies. In Paradise the fruits were ripe the first minute, and in Heaven it is always autumn, His mercies are ever in their maturity.

God goes forward in His own ways, and proceeds as he began, in mercy. One of the most convenient hyroglyphics of God is a circle, and a circle is endless. Whom God loves He loves to the end; and not only to their own end, to their death, but to His end; and His end is, that He might love them still.

God is a circle, and He will make thee one; go not thou about to square either circle, to bring that which is equal in itself to angles and corners, into dark and sad suspicions of God, or of thyself: that God can give, or that thou canst receive, no more of mercy than thou hast already.

As the sun doth not set to any nation, but withdraws itself and returns again, so God, in the exercise of His mercy, doth not set to thy soul, though He benight it with an affliction. The blessed Virgin was overshadowed, but it was with the Holy Ghost. Thine understanding, thy conscience may be so too, and yet it may be the work of the Holy Ghost, Who moves in thy darkness and will bring light even out of that, will bring knowledge out of thine ignorance, clearness out of thy scruples, and consolation out of thy dejection of spirit. The sun is not weary with so many thousand years shining; God cannot be weary of doing good.

"God is thy portion," says David. David does not speak so narrowly, so penuriously as to say, God hath given thee thy portion, and thou must look for no more. But, "God is thy portion," and as long as He is God He hath more to give, and as long as thou art His, thou hast more to receive.

John Donne
1573–1631

24

THE RAINBOW

And God said . . . I do set my bow in the cloud, and it shall be for a token of a covenant between me and the earth. And it shall come to pass, when I bring a cloud over the earth, that the bow shall be seen in the cloud. . . . While the earth remaineth, seedtime and harvest, and cold and heat, and summer and winter, and day and night shall not cease.

Genesis 9:12–14, 8:22

JESUS ANSWERS OUR NEED FOR LOVE

God loves you when you have done well. He's pleased when you've accomplished something worthwhile. But the good news is that He loves you even when you haven't done well. He loves you even when you mess up. He loves you when you've done terrible things. He loves you even when you've done the most despicable things imaginable. In spite of anything you might have done, God still loves you. In spite of what you are, God still loves you. That's what *agape* is all about. *Agape* love, unlike *eros*, is exceedingly stable. It is a never-ending love that never wavers or, to use the words of the Apostle Paul in 1 Corinthians 13, "Love never faileth." What is equally significant is that this *agape* love of God can flow through one person into the lives of others. Each of us is capable of becoming a conduit through which God's love is "shed abroad" for others to experience.

Anthony Campolo

Love has strong arms. Strong enough to steady my step if I slip, to take hold of my shivering heart and restore its steady rhythm. Love's arms lift me up and set me high upon a rock.

From that holy vantage point wicked men look insignificant, which, says love, they are! Love ought to know, because love is God.

Jill Briscoe

THE MAGNIFICENCE OF GOD'S LOVE

The measure of God's love is impossible to gauge with human instruments. In Matthew 5:45 Jesus said, ". . . he maketh his sun to rise on the evil and on the good, and sendeth rain on the just and on the unjust." What does that have to do with love? Look at verse 48: "Be ye therefore perfect, even as your Father which is in heaven is perfect." We could substitute the word "mature" there for "perfect," which is closer to what Jesus is saying. He's not talking about sinless perfection—he's talking about love, about kindness, about a maturity in God that is broader than mere human language can convey. Unbelievable as it may seem, this magnificence of God's love is intended to be worked out in the lives of God's children.

There is such a thing as family likeness. How common it is for us to say that a son is the "image of his father" and a daughter is "as lovely as her mother." Our human minds sometimes find it difficult if not impossible to grasp the implications of human likeness, but how much more mind-boggling is this matter of divine likeness. We are to be like our heavenly Father—that's what Jesus is saying here. And one of the most striking ways we can show this likeness is through sharing the love of God.

D. Stuart Briscoe

Love is the greatest thing that God can give us, for Himself is Love; and it is the greatest thing we can give to God, for it will also give ourselves, and carry with it all that is ours. Let our love be firm, constant, and inseparable; not coming and returning like the tide, but descending like a never-failing river, ever running into the ocean of Divine excellency, passing on in the channels of duty and a constant obedience, and never ceasing to be what it is, till it comes to what it desires to be; still being a river till it be turned into a sea, and vastness, even the immensity of a blessed eternity.

Bishop Jeremy Taylor
1613–1667

THE QUINTESSENCE OF GOD'S LOVE

As Jesus Christ was the perfect manifestation of God and His love, so is encouragement the perfect human expression of that love.

We must strive for, pant for, and long to express God's love to others as we live on this earth. Do you ever read the comic section of the newspaper? As Garfield goes after his plate of lasagna, as Linus clutches his blanket, and as Lolly's boss hangs on his golf clubs, so must we embrace encouragement as the means of expressing God's love through us to the people in our lives.

Encouragement is a precious gift in which we give of ourselves to one another. It is alive. It burrows itself down into our hearts and pierces our spirits. It moves us. It stirs us. It prods us. It changes our thinking, builds our self-esteem, and reveals to us the extent of God's love and the ever-present hope of knowing Him in all His fullness.

Encouragement is open-ended and unlimited. It will never lie to us by telling us we have already arrived but it will always expect the best from us. Encouragement is real. It touches us. It holds us in a warm embrace.

Encouragement is a gift from God that must be opened and used. It supersedes human compassion, for it is of God. It transcends human understanding, for can we fully explain God? Only He knows why you cry. Only He knows your deepest spiritual needs.

It is only as we yield ourselves to the Lord, for His use, that He can employ the precious gift of encouragement to meet our innermost needs.

To think that God would trust us with such a treasure.
What really happens when we encourage?
Abundant life.

Gloria Chisholm

PETER: THE GREATNESS OF LOVE

Peter was grieved because He said unto him the third time,
Lovest thou Me? He said unto Him, Lord, Thou knowest all
things; Thou knowest that I love Thee. Jesus saith unto him,
Feed My sheep (John xxi.17).

It was Mary who loved much that Christ first revealed
Himself. Then in Peter's first vision of the Lord, in His making Himself known in the upper room at Emmaus, in His
appearance to the ten, and in the revelation of Himself to
Thomas, it was ever to the intense devotion of the prepared
heart that Christ manifested Himself. And now in His manifestation of Himself to Peter it is again love that is the key-
note.

We can easily understand why Christ asked the question
thrice, Lovest thou Me? It was to remind Peter of the terrible
self-confidence in which he had said: "Though I should die
with Thee, I will not deny Thee"; of the need of quiet, deep
heart-searching ere he could be sure that his love was real and
true; of the need of deep penitence in the consciousness of
how little he could trust himself; and then of love being the
one thing needful for the full restoration to his place in
the heart of Jesus, the first and highest condition for feeding
His sheep and caring for His lambs.

God is love. Christ is the Son of His love. Having loved His
own, He loved them to the uttermost, and said: "As the Father
loved Me, so love I you." He asked that they should prove their
love to Him by keeping His commandments and loving each
other with the love with which He loved them. In heaven and
on earth, in the Father and in the Son, and in us, and in all our
work for Him and our care for souls, the greatest thing is love.

To everyone who longs to have Jesus manifest Himself—"I

am with you alway"—the chief, the essential requisite is love. Peter teaches us that such love is not in the power of man to offer. But such love came to him through the power of Christ's death to sin, and that power of His resurrection life, of which Peter became partaker. As he puts it in his first Epistle: "Whom having not seen, we love; in Whom, though now ye see Him not, yet believing, ye rejoice with joy unspeakable and full of glory." Thank God, if Peter the self-confident could be so changed, shall not we believe that Christ will work in us the wondrous change too, and manifest Himself to a loving heart in all the fullness of His precious word: "Lo, I am with you alway." It is to love that Christ will manifest Himself, as the only fitness for feeding His sheep and tending His lambs.

Andrew Murray

WHEN GOD SAYS NO

A young pastor friend has in this last year been through the trial of his life. When I saw him recently, he asked me, "What do you do when God doesn't say yes—doesn't give it, doesn't make it happen?" Then he answered his own question: "Through agony I've gotten to know God better; I love him more. . . ."

He showed me a piece of paper he keeps in his wallet. It says, "Look to his face, not to his hand."

But all this is not to say that God very often answers us with no! Be encouraged that he loves his children, and he loves to say yes! He can synchronize your heart with his, and empower you to ask the enormous things that delight him to answer—and delight you, too.

He opens himself up to you in Jeremiah 33:3: "Call unto me, and I will answer thee, and shew thee great and mighty things, which thou knowest not."

And he offers you in Matthew 7:7,8 a powerful acrostic:

> **A**sk and it will be given to you:
> **S**eek and you will find;
> **K**nock and the door will be opened to you.

And who but God himself can explain this dynamic, sweeping conclusion: "For everyone who asks receives; he who seeks finds; and to him who knocks, the door will be opened"?!

The question we have to ask ourselves is, *what is it we really want?*

If we want just an ordinary life, God will give us that. If we want to hang onto our personal sins at any cost, God honors the free will he gave us. We'll just miss all the fun and all the rewards.

Anne Ortlund

This prayer was found in an old book, the faded handwriting barely visible:

By thy forgiving tenderness, O Lord, wherewith thou didst ever wait for us; by that tender love wherewith whenever we wandered, thou didst watch over us; by thine infinite love wherewith thou willest that we should love thee eternally; Give us love like thine, that we may glow in thy love, and dwelling in love may dwell in Thee.

— 2 —

The Love that changes our lives
teaches us how to love.

I love, my God, but with no love of mine,
    For I have none to give;
I love Thee, Lord, but all the love is Thine,
    For by Thy life I live.
I am as nothing, and rejoice to be
Emptied and lost and swallowed up by Thee.

Thou, Lord, alone art all Thy children need,
    And there is none beside;
From Thee the streams of blessedness proceed;
    In Thee the blest abide,
Fountain of life, and all-abounding grace,
Our source, our center, and our dwelling place!

Madam Jeanne Marie Guyon
1648–1717

JESUS' LOVE FOR THOSE HE TAUGHT

"One loving spirit," said St. Augustine, "set another one fire"; and that was and is the ultimate secret of Christ's divine success as Teacher. From His loving spirit the spirits of His pupils were continually catching fire, so that the lesson, in that flame of mutual love, was no dreary discipline, but joy and romance and glory. Bungling pupils in Christ's school the disciples often were, disappointing Him sorely at a score of points and stumbling sadly over His great lesson of faith and hope and love. And yet, for all the sorry show they made in these things, their love to Him was growing all the time. His loving spirit was triumphing over all the hindrances in them. And a day came (it was after Calvary and Pentecost) when at long last they had their lesson—the great central message of redemption—perfect and complete and without any flaw at all; and went forth to proclaim it to the earth.

James S. Stewart

Everything that is tender, that is sensitive, that is movingly beautiful in modernity, comes from Christ.

Edmond and Jules de Goncourt
1867

HEALING A BROKEN WORLD

Professor Henry Drummond in one of his remarkable essays makes the statement that true Christianity, true love, true "selflessness" does its own delightful healing, saving work in secret. Then it steals away in silence, unseen, forgetting, even its own lowly, winsome touch upon the life of another.

Our Lord made much of this principle in His teaching. He pointed out the unnoticed widow who gave all she had in her two tiny mites of money. He told the story of the poor, contrite publican praying unheard, unseen in his quiet corner. He recounted the stirring saga of the shepherd who alone, unsung, in the wilderness, rescued one wandering sheep. These were His heroes. These were the "great" ones in His estimation who by the world's standards were second-rate people.

Salt is not showy! Salt is not spectacular! Salt is not strident! It is simple. It is silent. Yet it is special in its healing qualities.

Only rarely, here and there, does God ever call a man or woman to special display or dramatic demonstrations. Much more often He simply asks us to be those silent, sincere souls who in service to Him and those around us help to heal a hurting, broken world.

We can bring to this sick world honest work, inspiring hope, good cheer, lofty ideals, a helping hand, a warm heart, a shining smile, a word of encouragement, a friendly hug, a share of ourselves.

Because we have been here some broken heart, some broken home or some broken hope will have been healed. And even God will be glad.

W. Phillip Keller

Let every man be swift to hear, slow to speak, slow to wrath (S. James i.19).

Kind words are the music of the world. They have a power which seems to be beyond natural causes, as if they were some angel's song which had lost its way, and come on earth. It seems as if they could almost do what in reality God alone can do, soften the hard and angry hearts of men. No one was ever corrected by a sarcasm; crushed perhaps if the sarcasm was clever enough, but drawn nearer to God, never.

Frederick William Faber
1814–1863

You will find as you look back upon your life that the moments that stand out, the moments when you have really lived, are the moments when you have done things in a spirit of love. As memory scans the past, above and beyond all the transitory pleasures of life, there leap forward those supreme hours when you have been enabled to do unnoticed kindnesses to those round about you, things too trifling to speak about, but which you feel have entered into your eternal life. I have seen almost all the beautiful things God has made; I have enjoyed almost every pleasure that He has planned for man; and yet as I look back I see standing out above all the life that has gone, four or five short experiences when the love of God reflected itself in some poor imitation, some small act of love of mine, and these seem to be the things which alone of all one's life abide. Everything else in all our lives is transitory. Every other good is visionary. But the acts of love which no man knows about, or can ever know about—they never fail.

Henry Drummond
1851–1897

TRUE POWER

If we would love God, we must love His justice and act upon it. Then, taking a holy, radical stand—*contra mundum* if need be—we surrender the illusion of power and find it replaced by True Power. That was certainly one of Alexander Solzhenitsyn's greatest discoveries in the Soviet gulag.

Like other prisoners, Solzhenitsyn worked in the fields, his days a pattern of backbreaking labor and slow starvation. One day the hopelessness became too much to bear. Solzhenitsyn felt no purpose in fighting on; his life would make no ultimate difference. Laying his shovel down, he walked slowly to a crude work-site bench. He knew at any moment a guard

34

would order him up and, when he failed to respond, bludgeon him to death, probably with his own shovel. He'd seen it happen many times.

As he sat waiting, head down, he felt a presence. Slowly he lifted his eyes. Next to him sat an old man with a wrinkled, utterly expressionless face. Hunched over, the old man drew a stick through the sand at Solzhenitsyn's feet, deliberately tracing out the sign of the cross.

As Solzhenitsyn stared at that rough outline, his entire perspective shifted. He knew he was merely one man against the all-powerful Soviet empire. Yet in that moment, he also knew that the hope of all mankind was represented by that simple cross—and through its power, anything was possible. Solzhenitsyn slowly got up, picked up his shovel, and went back to work—not knowing that his writings on truth and freedom would one day enflame the whole world.

Such is the power God's truth affords one man willing to stand against hopeless odds. Such is the power of the cross.

Charles W. Colson

I love you, Lord, not doubtingly, but with absolute certainty. Your Word beat upon my heart until I fell in love with you, and now the universe and everything in it tells me to love you, and tells the same thing to us all, so that we are without excuse.

And what do I love when I love you? Not physical beauty, or the grandeur of our existence in time, or the radiance of light that pleases the eye, or the sweet melody of old familiar songs, or the fragrance of flowers and ointments and spices, or the taste of manna or honey, or the arms we like to use to clasp each other. None of these do I love when I love my God. Yet there is a kind of light, and a kind of melody, and a kind of fragrance, and a kind of food, and a kind of embracing, when I love my God. They are the kind of light and sound and odor and food and love that affect the senses of my inner man. There is another dimension of life in which my soul reflects a light that space itself cannot contain. It hears melodies that never fade with time. It inhales lovely scents that are not

blown away by the wind. It eats without diminishing or con-
suming the supply. It never gets separated from the embrace
of God and never gets tired of it. That is what I love when I
love my God.

Saint Augustine
A.D. 354–430
(translated by Sherwood E. Wirt)

. . . Love will teach us all things: but we must learn how to
win love; it is got with difficulty: it is a possession dearly
bought with much labour and in a long time; for one must love
not sometimes only, for a passing moment, but always. There
is no man who doth not sometimes love: even the wicked can
do that.

And let not men's sin dishearten thee: love a man even in
his sin, for that love is a likeness of the divine love, and is
the summit of love on earth. Love all God's creation, both the
whole and every grain of sand. Love every leaf, every ray of
light. Love the animals, love the plants, love each separate
thing. If thou love each thing thou wilt perceive the mystery
of God in all; and when once thou perceive this, thou wilt
thenceforward grow every day to a fuller understanding of it:
until thou come at least to love the whole world with a love
that will then be all-embracing and universal.

Fyodor Dostoevsky
(from *The Brothers Karamazov*)

There was a time when Jesus was asked this question:
"Which is the greatest commandment of the Law?" He replied,
"You must love the Lord your God with all your heart, soul,
mind, and strength. The second is this: "You must love your
neighbor as yourself. There is no commandment greater, and
on these the whole law is based." Then, at the Last Supper He
said: "This is my commandment, love one another as I have

loved you. A man can have no greater love than to lay down his life for his friends." When we tie these three commandments together, it sums up in real terms what God expects of us and what Jesus Christ did for us; and therein lies the basis of the Gospel and our guide to life. If we can implant these thoughts in our minds, life will take on new meaning and will be uncomplicated because Jesus Christ did not want the word of God complicated. In fact, he made it simple enough to be revealing to little children. We need to accept His word with the simplicity and the trust of a child-like heart.

Anthony G. Bottagaro

Helen Keller's great faith continues to illuminate our world. In her book, Midstream, *she wrote of her unswerving belief in God's will for each one of us:*

I believe that we can live on earth according to the teachings of Jesus, and that the greatest happiness will come to the world when man obeys His commandment "Love ye one another."

I believe that every question between man and man is a religious question, and that every social wrong is a moral wrong.

I believe that we can live on earth according to the fulfillment of God's will, and that when the will of God is done on earth as it is done in heaven, every man will love his fellow men, and act towards them as he desires they should act towards him. I believe that the welfare of each is bound up in the welfare of all.

I believe that life is given us so we may grow in love, and I believe that God is in me as the sun is in the colour and fragrance of a flower—the Light in my darkness, the Voice in my silence.

I believe that only in broken gleams has the Sun of Truth yet shone upon men. I believe that love will finally establish the Kingdom of God on earth, and that the Cornerstones of that Kingdom will be Liberty, Truth, Brotherhood, and Service.

I believe that no good shall be lost, and that all man has willed or hoped or dreamed of good shall exist forever.

I believe in the immortality of the soul because I have within me immortal longings. I believe that the state we enter after death is wrought of our own motives, thoughts, and deeds. I believe that in the life to come I shall have the senses I have not had here, and that my home there will be beautiful with colour, music, and speech of flowers and faces I love.

Without this faith there would be little meaning in my life. I should be "a mere pillar of darkness in the dark." Observers in the full enjoyment of their bodily senses pity me, but it is because they do not see the golden chamber in my life where I dwell delighted; for, dark as my path may seem to them, I carry a magic light in my heart. Faith, the spiritual strong searchlight, illumines the way, and although sinister doubts lurk in the shadow, I walk unafraid towards the Enchanted Wood where the foliage is always green, where joy abides, where nightingales nest and sing, and where life and death are one in the Presence of the Lord.

Helen Keller

How valuable to *you* are relationships? If you have trouble answering that, I'll help you decide. Stop and think back over the past month or two. How much of your leisure have you spent developing and enjoying relationships?

Jesus, God's Son, certainly considered the relationship He had with His disciples worth His time. They spent literally *hours* together. They ate together and wept together, and I'm sure they must have laughed together as well. Being God, He really didn't "need" those men. He certainly did not need the hassle they created on occasion. But He loved those twelve men. He believed in them. They had a special relationship—a lot like Paul, Silas, and Timothy; David and Jonathan; Barnabas and John Mark; Elijah and Elisha.

As the poet Samuel Taylor Coleridge once put it, "Friendship is a sheltering tree." How very true! Whatever leisure time we are able to invest in relationships is time well spent. And when we do, let's keep in mind we are "imitating God," for His Son certainly did.

Charles R. Swindoll

A NEW CHURCH FOR A NEW DAY

It is love, vulnerable and affirmative, which is the genius of the whole Christian experiment. This is the mark of the new kind of society called "the Church" or "the Body of Christ" which God came into the world to create.

In this society, we are to experience relationships—and to become those who because Christ is in us can become relatable to others. . . . A glimpse of what the new Church might look like can be seen in a letter from a teenager whom I don't know personally, but who lives in the deep South. Here is what she says:

"My campaigners leader suggested that I write to you about the neat thing that happened to me last week. Jan asked us what one thing we wouldn't do without Christ in our lives. One of the many things I wouldn't do is tell my father I love him.

"I prayed that afternoon and that night and the next day at school that Christ would first give me the will to tell my father how much I love him and then to make me do it.

"My parents love me a great deal, and I love them, too. I have always been pretty close to my mother, but my father and I have always been distant. I felt as if he didn't think I loved him. Telling someone I love them is the hardest thing I have ever done, and I know it would be impossible without Christ. . . ."

She then goes on to tell about praying for the courage to go to her father and tell him what he had meant to her over the years. And one day she left school early and went to her father's office, just to tell him this one thing. There were tears and laughter and a new relationship between the two of them.

It seems to me that this is the kind of thing that the Church is all about. Because of the dynamic of Jesus Christ and His love for us, we become released to tell people how much 'they mean to us—to affirm them, to become vulnerable even with a parent or a spouse, let alone a stranger.

Bruce Larson

THE CHARITY TEST

The human being who has opened to God's touch will be made more God-like by reason of that contact. He will become more loving. St. John says that God is love and that anyone who fails to love cannot have known God. He who abides in God abides in love. The grandest, most glowing of all God's miraculous interventions will always be the production of a loving person, the transformation of a go-getter into a go-giver. Essentially, this is what the hours or touches of God are all about. This is what God is doing. The gift of love is the highest gift of the Spirit.

John Powell

We love wherever we can love, and the power of that love spreads until the circumference of the circle of love grows wider and wider. At least that has been my own experience, even though I know to my rue that the circumference of my life is still much too small.

It's too small for all of us; I'm not just breast beating. The circle grows slowly and painfully even with the saints, and so does purity of heart. Who can possibly be pure of heart in this impure world?

Peter. Peter recognized Jesus as the Messiah, the Christ. And Jesus said, "Flesh and blood has not told you this." So purity of heart is not a virtue, it is a gift, and Peter, bumbling, noisy Peter, was given the gift of purity, the ability to see God. And after this he betrayed the God he had seen, he ran from him, he denied him, he was not there when they crucified his Lord. But he believed in the Resurrection, and his confession of Jesus as Messiah was the rock on which the Church was founded, and in the end he lay down his life for what he had seen and known.

The fact that Peter could see God, and thus be pure in heart despite all his faults and flaws, is a great comfort, because it tells me that this purity, like every single one of the Beatitudes, is available to each of us, a sheer gift of grace, if we are willing to be vulnerable.

Madeleine L'Engle

You shall love your neighbor as yourself.

Matthew 22:39 NKJV

We have hearts with over 100,000 miles of veins and arteries running throughout our bodies. Our hearts pump blood throughout that 100,000-mile course many times per day. According to one scientist, one pound of human flesh, if broken down into its chemical components, would be worth $570,000,000. If we weigh 150 pounds, our flesh is worth over $85,000,000,000. This means that each of us is infinitely valuable! As the psalmist said, we are "fearfully and wonderfully made" (Ps. 139:14).

Our brain is the most amazing instrument of all! It has over ten billion nerve cells. Even thousands of gigantic microcomputers cannot duplicate what one human brain can do, because no computer can program itself. Our brains *can* program themselves, and they can hold fantastic quantities of data.

If you were to add one bit of information to your memory banks every second for seventy years, you would only use a small fraction of the storage capacity in the brain which God has given you. At sixty seconds in a minute, sixty minutes in an hour, twenty-four hours in a day, seven days in a week, and fifty-two weeks in a year, that would be 2,201,472,000 bits of information! The human brain is a real marvel.

To think about that is exciting because it means God cared enough about us to give us this special capacity. He didn't have to, but he must have given it to us for a reason. Surely he didn't give us that fantastic thinking ability for it to remain unused.

We would urge you to repeat these words daily until you accept them as fact: "I'm fantastic because God made me with the ability to absorb some new bit of information every second of every minute of every hour of every day of every week of every year for my entire life. He must have given me that capacity to use." Then ask, "Well, what use did he intend for me?" There must be some good reason for all that ability.

Bill Glass and James E. McEachern

Are you lonely, O my brother?
    Share your little with another!
Stretch your hand to one unfriended,
    And your loneliness is ended.

John Oxenham

So deep and meaningful is the joy and the enthusiasm that is born in one's mind and heart by human love and helpfulness that it has the power to motivate for a lifetime.

A physician well on in years told me how he became a doctor. His story was so wonderful that I never forgot it. He told me that, as a small boy, he lived with his parents in Kansas, in a district where, in wintertime, the countryside often lay under deep drifted snow and there would be difficulty getting in and out between town and his family's farm.

One winter when he was about seven years old, his little sister got sick, ran a high fever, became delirious. By the time his father got a message over the well-nigh impassable roads to the doctor, and the doctor finally arrived, with horse and buggy breaking through the snow, the little girl was sick unto death. The doctor remained for twenty-four hours until the crisis was passed. The whole household was in anguish. No one had a minute's sleep.

Finally the little boy saw the doctor walk across the room

and put his hands on the shoulders of his father and mother, and heard him say to them, "By the grace of God, I am happy to tell you that little Mary will get well." The boy, from where he stood crouching behind a chair, could see his parents' faces in that moment. He had never seen them so beautiful, so lighted up, so wonderfully happy. They had been made that way by what the doctor had said to them.

"Right in that moment," my friend concluded, "I decided I was going to be a doctor, so I could say things like that to people that would bring that light to their eyes, that joy to their faces."

You don't have to be a doctor to say or do that which puts light in a human eye and joy on a human face. Simply practice Jesus' commandment that we love one another. Go out and do something for somebody. These are the things that make happy people happy. "If ye know these things, happy are ye if ye do them" (John 13:17). Here is the one never-failing source of the joy and enthusiasm we are talking about.

No wonder that Christianity, which teaches the way to happy life, emphasizes and underscores love. Three great words there are—*faith, hope, love;* but the greatest of the three greatest words in the English language, or, indeed, any language, is *love.* And "Love never fails . . ." (1 Corinthians 13:8, NKJV). Saint John says:

> Greater love hath no man than this, that a man lay down his life for his friends (John 15:13).

> And this commandment have we from him, That he who loveth God love his brother also (1 John 4:21).

Norman Vincent Peale

O God, who hast prepared for them that love thee such good things as pass man's understanding: Pour into our hearts such love toward thee, that we, loving thee above all things, may obtain thy promises, which exceed all that we can desire: through Jesus Christ our Lord. Amen.

Book of Common Prayer

~⟡ *Part Two* ⟡~

Created to Love Him

⚜ 3 ⚜

*Worship is a glorious avenue for
our expression of love for God.*

I remember running over the hills
    just at dawn one summer morning and,
pausing to rest in the silent woods, saw, through an arch of trees,
    the sun rise over river, hill,
      and wide green meadows as I never saw it before.
Something born of the lovely hour, a happy mood,
  and the unfolding aspirations of a child's soul
    seemed to bring me very near to God. . . .

Louisa May Alcott
1832–1888

It was early in the morning in another country. Exhausted as I was, I awoke around three o'clock. The name of someone I loved dearly flashed into my mind. It was like an electric shock. Instantly I was wide-awake. I knew there would be no more sleep for me the rest of the night. So I lay there and prayed for the one who was trying hard to run away from God. When it is dark and the imagination runs wild, there are fears that only a mother can understand.

Suddenly the Lord said to me, *Quit studying the problems and start studying the promises.* Now God has never spoken to me audibly, but there is no mistaking when He speaks.

So I turned on the light, got out my Bible, and the first verse that came to me was Philippians 4:6: "Be careful for nothing; but in every thing by prayer and supplication *with thanksgiving* let your requests be made known unto God." And verse 7: "And the peace of God, which passeth all understanding, shall keep your hearts and minds through Christ Jesus." Or, as the Amplified Version has it, "Do not fret or have any anxiety about anything, but in every circumstance and in everything by prayer and petition (definite requests) *with thanksgiving* continue to make your wants known to God . . ." (my italics).

Suddenly I realized the missing ingredient in my prayers had been "with thanksgiving." So I put down my Bible and spent time worshiping Him for who He is and what He is. This covers more territory than any one mortal can comprehend. Even contemplating what little we do know dissolves doubts, reinforces faith, and restores joy. I began to thank God for giving me this one I loved so dearly in the first place. I even thanked Him for the difficult spots which taught me so much.

And you know what happened? It was as if suddenly someone turned on the lights in my mind and heart, and the little fears and worries which, like mice and cockroaches, had been nibbling away in the darkness, suddenly scuttled for cover.

That was when I learned that worship and worry cannot live in the same heart: they are mutually exclusive.

Ruth Bell Graham

The prayers I make will then be sweet indeed,
  If Thou the spirit give by which I pray;
  My unassisted heart is barren clay,
Which of its native self can nothing feed;
Of good and pious works Thou art the seed
  Which quickens where Thou say'st it may;
  Unless Thou show us then Thine own true way,
No man can find it! Father, Thou must lead!
Do Thou, then, breathe those thoughts into my mind
  By which such virtue may in me be bred
  That in Thy holy footsteps I may tread:
The fetters of my tongue do Thou unbind,
  That I may have the power to sing of Thee
  And sound Thy praises everlastingly.

Michelangelo
(translated by William Wordsworth)

Awake my soul, and with the sun
Thy daily stage of duty run;
Shake off dull sloth, and joyful rise
To pay the morning sacrifice!

Shine on me, Lord, new life impart,
Fresh ardors kindle in my heart;
One ray of Thine all-quickening light
Dispels the clouds and dark of night.

Thomas Ken
1637–1711

Give ear to my words, O Lord, consider my meditation. Hearken unto the voice of my cry. . . . My voice shalt thou hear in the morning, O Lord; in the morning will I direct my prayer unto thee, and will look up (Psalm 5:1–3).

God, who created heaven and earth, will hear *my* voice? The King of the universe will consider *my* meditation? Oh, thank You, Lord, for the undreamed-of opportunity of this audience with the King! Anyone who has a favor to ask of an earthly monarch has no chance of having his request granted until he makes his wish known to the king. That *could* be second-hand—generally is, in protocol-bound human societies. What a privilege to have an audience in person! Yet this is the status and the honor You allow each of us, Lord.

Even more privileged is he so in favor with the King that he is allowed as long as he wishes to be with the One he loves, listen to Him, watch Him, bask in His presence. In earthly courts, such a one would be considered favored indeed, and the courts we're invited to enter are of an "infinite majesty." Just to say "Thank You" seems inadequate. This morning I make it a welling, swelling gratitude!

Catherine Marshall

Be not forgetful of prayer.
    Every time you pray, if your prayer is sincere,
there will be new feeling and new meaning in it,
    which will give you fresh courage,
    and you will understand that prayer is an education.

Fyodor Dostoevsky

THE DAY'S BEGINNING

"Let the word of Christ dwell in you richly" (Col. 3:16). The Old Testament day begins at evening and ends with the going down of the sun. It is the time of expectation. The day of the

New Testament church begins with the break of day and ends with the dawning light of the next morning. It is the time of fulfillment, the resurrection of the Lord. At night Christ was born, a light in darkness; noonday turned to night when Christ suffered and died on the Cross. But in the dawn of Easter morning Christ rose in victory from the grave.

> Ere yet the dawn hath filled the skies
> Behold my Savior Christ arise,
> He chaseth from us sin and night,
> And brings us joy and life and light.
> Hallellujah

So sang the church of the Reformation. Christ is the "Sun of righteousness," risen upon the expectant congregation (Mal. 4:2), and they that love him shall "be as the sun when he goeth forth in his might" (Judges 5:31). The early morning belongs to the Church of the risen Christ. At the break of light it remembers the morning on which death and sin lay prostrate in defeat and new life and salvation were given to mankind.

Dietrich Bonhoeffer

Praise ye the Lord.
  Praise, O ye servants of the Lord,
  praise the name of the Lord.
Blessed be the name of the Lord
  from this time forth and for evermore.
From the rising of the sun unto the going down of the same
  the Lord's name is to be praised.
The Lord is high above all nations,
  and his glory above the heavens.
Who is like unto the Lord our God,
  who dwelleth on high.
Who humbled himself to behold
  the things that are in heaven, and in the earth!

Psalm 113:1-6

SONNET

Oft I have seen at some cathedral door
　A laborer, pausing in the dust and heat,
　lay down his burden, and with reverent feet
　Enter and cross himself, and on the floor
Kneel to repeat his paternoster o'er;
　Far off the noises of the world retreat;
　The loud vociferations of the street
　Become an undistinguishable roar.
So, as I enter here from day to day,
　And leave my burden at this minster gate,
　Kneeling in prayer, and not ashamed to pray,
The tumult of the time disconsolate
　To inarticulate murmurs dies away,
　While the eternal ages watch and wait.

Henry Wadsworth Longfellow

The uplift of adoration brings the humble but blessed beholder to the threshold of a worship which miraculously transforms him just by beholding.

Out of the horrors of the second world war came an expression of such worship—a poem written by a nineteen-year-old flyer who met his death serving with the Royal Canadian Air Force. His father was an Episcopal rector whom I knew in Washington.

Pilot-Officer John Gillespie Magee, Jr., called his poem "High Flight . . ."

Oh, I have slipped the surly bonds of earth,
And danced the skies on laughter-silvered wings.
Sunward I've climbed, and joined the tumbling mirth
Of sun-split clouds—and done a hundred things
You have not dreamed of—wheeled and soared and swung

52

High on the sunlit silence. Hov'ring there,
I've chased the shouting wind along, and flung
My eager craft through footless halls of air.

Up, up the long, delirious, burning blue,
I've topped the windswept heights with easy grace
Where never lark, or even eagle flew—
And, while with silent, lifting mind I've trod
The high untrespassed sanctity of space,
Put out my hand and touched the face of God.

The Christian is to seek the things above—to seek them
    as the needle seeks the pole . . .
    as the sunflower seeks the sun . . .
    as the river seeks the sea . . .
    as the eagle seeks the ceiling of the world.
That was why Paul pleaded with the first-century Christians to set their affections on things above . . .
                    high things,
                    lofty concepts
and "not on the things of the earth."

                        Peter Marshall

O Lord our Lord,
    how excellent is thy name in all the earth!
    who has set thy glory above the heavens.
Out of the mouth of babes and sucklings
    hast thou ordained strength
    because of thine enemies,
    that thou mightest still the enemy and the avenger.
When I consider thy heavens, the work of thy fingers,
    the moon and the stars, which thou hast ordained:
What is man, that thou art mindful of him?
    and the son of man, that thou visitest him?
For thou hast made him a little lower than the angels,
    and hast crowned him with glory and honour.
Thou madest him to have dominion over the works of thy
       hands;

thou hast put all things under his feet:
All sheep and oxen, yea,
   and the beasts of the field;
The fowl of the air, and the fish of the sea,
   and whatsoever passeth through the paths of the seas.
O Lord our Lord,
   how excellent is thy name in all the earth.

Psalm 8

THE QUIET ROOM

And so I find it well to come
For deeper rest to this still room;
For here the habit of the soul
Feels less the outer world's control.
And from the silence, multiplied
By these still forms on every side,
The world that time and sense has known
Falls off and leaves us God alone.

John Greenleaf Whittier
1807–1892

THE STARS

If a man would be alone, let him look at the stars. The rays that come from those heavenly worlds will separate between him and what he touches.

One might think the atmosphere was made transparent with this design, to give man, in the heavenly bodies, the perpetual presence of the sublime. Seen in the streets of cities, how great they are!

If the stars should appear one night in a thousand years, how would men believe, and adore, and preserve for many generations, the remembrance of the city of God which had been shown? But every night come out these envoys of beauty, and light the universe with their admonishing smile.

Ralph Waldo Emerson

For a full day and two nights I have been alone. I lay on the beach under the stars at night alone. I made my breakfast alone. Alone I watched the gulls at the end of the pier, dip and wheel and dive for the scraps I threw them. A morning's work at my desk, and then, a late picnic lunch alone on the beach. And it seemed to me, separated from my own species, that I was nearer to others: the shy willet, nesting in the ragged tide-wash behind me; the sand piper, running in little unfrightened steps down the shining beach rim ahead of me; the slowly flapping pelicans over my head, coasting down wind; the old gull, hunched up, grouchy, surveying the horizon. I felt a kind of impersonal kinship with them and a joy in that kinship. Beauty of earth and sea and air meant more to me. I was in harmony with it, melted into the universe, lost in it, as one is lost in a canticle of praise, swelling from an unknown crowd in a cathedral. "Praise ye the Lord, all ye fishes of the sea—all ye birds of the air—all ye children of men—Praise ye the Lord!"

Anne Morrow Lindbergh

Let us with gladsome mind
Praise the Lord, for He is kind:
For His mercies shall endure,
Ever faithful, ever sure.

John Milton
1608–1674

WHEN THE WINDS CRY I HEAR YOU

Oh God, my God, when the winds cry I hear you, when the birds call I hear you, when the sea rushes in it is like the rushing of my being toward yours.

You are voice of wind and bird and beat of sea. You are the silent steady pulsing of my blood.

I would know you better, I would taste your essence, I would see your face.

Yet these few small senses of mine cannot do more. You have defined their limits, you have set them within a framework from which we can only see and touch and hear and attempt to know these marvels that you have made.

But this too is the marvel—that you are within each of us as well. As we are drawn toward your greatness we are drawn toward the greatness within ourselves.

We are larger beings, we are greater spirits.

The hunger for you kindles a holy fire that makes us kinder, gentler, surer, stronger—ever seeking, never quite finding, but always keenly aware that you are all about us and within us.

You are here.

Marjorie Holmes

As flowers carry dewdrops, trembling on the edges of the petals, and ready to fall at the first waft of the wind or brush of bird, so that heart should carry its beaded words of thanksgiving. At the first breath of heavenly flavor, let down the shower, perfumed with the heart's gratitude.

Henry Ward Beecher

It was inevitable, I suppose, that in the garden I should begin, at long last, to ask myself what lay behind all this beauty.

56

When guests were gone and I had the flowers to myself, I was so happy that I wondered why at the same time I was haunted by a sense of emptiness. It was as though I wanted to thank somebody, but had nobody to thank; which is another way of saying that I felt the need for worship. That is, perhaps, the kindliest way in which a man may come to his God. There is an interminable literature on the origins of the religious impulse, but to me it is simpler than that. It is summed up in the image of a man at sundown, watching the crimson flowering of the sky and saying—to somebody—"Thank you."

Beverley Nichols

Doth not all nature around me praise God? If I were silent, I should be an exception to the universe. Doth not the thunder praise Him as it rolls like drums in the march of the God of armies? Do not the mountains praise Him when the woods upon their summits wave in adoration? Does not the lightning write His name in letters of fire? Hath not the whole earth a voice? And shall I, can I, silent be?

Charles H. Spurgeon

The fact of Jesus Christ is the eternal message of the Bible. It is the story of life, peace, eternity, and heaven. The Bible has no hidden purpose. It has no need for special interpretation. It has a single, clear, bold message for every living being—the message of Christ and His offer of peace with God.

One day upon a mountain near Capernaum Jesus sat with His disciples. They gathered before Him—perhaps Peter on one side and John on the other. Jesus may have looked quietly and tenderly at each of these devoted disciples, looked at them the way a loving parent looks at the members of his family—loving each child separately, loving each for a special reason, loving them in such a way that each child feels singled out and individually embraced. That is how Jesus must have loved His disciples.

57

The little group must have become very reverent under His serene and loving gaze. They must have become very still within themselves with the feeling that something momentous was about to be said, something they must remember, something they must be able to transmit to others all over the world who were not privileged, as they were, to hear these words from the Master's own lips.

For there, on the mountain, standing perhaps under the silvery gray-green leaves of an olive tree, Jesus preached the greatest sermon that human ears have ever heard. He explained the essence of Christian living. When He was through and a holy hush had settled on His wide-eyed listeners, they "were astonished at his doctrine: for he taught them as one having authority, and not as the scribes" (Matthew 7:28, 29).

Indeed He did teach with authority, the authority of God Himself; and the rules He set forth were God's own rules, the ones which every Christian with the hope of salvation in his heart must follow.

Billy Graham

CRUSADER'S HYMN

Fairest Lord Jesus,
Ruler of all nature,
O Thou of God and man the Son,
Thee will I cherish, Thee will I honor,
Thou, my soul's glory, joy, and crown.

Fair are the meadows,
Fairer still the woodlands,
Robed in the blooming garb of spring;
Jesus is fairer, Jesus is purer,
Who makes the woeful heart to sing.

Fair is the sunshine,
Fairer still the moonlight,

And all the twinkling, starry host;
Jesus shines brighter, Jesus shines purer,
Than all the angels heaven can boast.

From the German, seventeenth century
(translated by R. Storrs Willis, c. 1850)

If Christ is the heart of the Old Testament, this is even more obvious in the New. The Gospels recount His earthly career, His virgin birth and sinless life, His gracious words and mighty works, His sinbearing death, His glorious resurrection and ascension. The book of Acts describes His gift of the Spirit on the Day of Pentecost, and what He continued to do and to teach by His Spirit through His apostles. The Epistles unfold more fully the unparalleled glory of His divine-human Person, saving work and coming kingdom, and tells us how we should live in the light of these truths. The Revelation lifts our eyes beyond earth and history, up to heaven where Christ is seen to share God's eternal throne and on to the end when He will come again in majesty, take His power and reign. Yet there are some people who read the whole Bible, New Testament as well as Old, without realizing that its principal purpose is to bear witness to Jesus Christ!

The Bible is full of Christ. Some of the old English commentators used to put it like this: Just as in England every road, lane and path, linking on to others, will ultimately lead you to London, so in the Bible every book, chapter and verse, linking on to others, will ultimately lead you to Christ.

John R. W. Stott

I know not the way He leads me,
but well I know my Guide.

Martin Luther

FROM THE EARLIEST CHRISTIAN HYMN

Shepherd and Sower, thou,
Now helm, and bridle now,
Wing for the heavenward flight
Of flocks all pure and bright,
Fisher of men, the blest,
Out of the world's unrest,
Out of Sin's troubled sea
Taking us, Lord, to thee . . .
O way that leads to God,
O Word abiding aye,
O endless Light on high,
Mercy's fresh-springing flood,
Worker of all things good,
O glorious Life of all,
That on their Maker call.
   Christ Jesus, hear . . .
Hymns meet for thee, our King,
   For thee, the Christ;
Our holy tribute, this,
For wisdom, life and bliss,
Singing in chorus meet,
Swinging in concert sweet
   The Almighty Son.
We, heirs of peace unpriced,
We, who are born in Christ,
A people pure from stain,
Praise we our God again,
   Lord of our Peace!

Clement of Alexandria
first century A.D.

THE NEED FOR GOD

When a man surveys his past from middle age he must surely ask himself what those bygone years have taught him. If I have learned anything in the swift unrolling of the web of time . . . it is the virtue of tolerance, of moderation in thought and deed, of forbearance toward one's fellowmen.

I have come also to acknowledge the great illusion which lies in the pursuit of a purely material goal. What slight satisfaction lies in temporal honour and worldly grandeur . . . ! All the material possessions for which I strove so strenuously mean less to me now than a glance of love from those who are dear to me.

Above all am I convinced of the need, irrevocable and inescapable, of every human heart, for God. No matter how we try to escape, to lose ourselves in restless seeking, we cannot separate ourselves from our divine source. There is no substitute for God.

A. J. Cronin

FROM *MARKINGS*

Offspring of the past, pregnant with the future,
the present moment, nevertheless, always exists
in eternity—always in eternity as the point
of intersection between time and the timelessness
of faith, and, therefore, as the moment of
freedom from past and future.

Thou who art over us,
Thou who art one of us,
Thou who *art* —
Also within us,
May all see Thee—in me also,

61

May I prepare the way for Thee,
May I thank Thee for all that shall fall to my lot,
May I also not forget the needs of others,
Keep me in Thy love
As thou wouldest that all should be kept in mine.
May everything in this my being be directed to Thy glory
And may I never despair
For I am under Thy hand,
And in Thee is all power and goodness.

Give me a pure heart—that I may see Thee,
A humble heart—that I may hear Thee,
A heart of love—that I may serve Thee,
A heart of faith—that I may abide in Thee.

Dag Hammarskjöld

A PERSON AFTER GOD'S HEART

David was a God-captivated man who wanted to please and serve his Lord above all else.

The dramatic episode of David's call and anointing by Samuel puts an exclamation point to the quality of heart God wanted in a new king for Israel. Jesse's older sons, all formidable specimens of manhood, were passed by Samuel's careful eye. As he evaluated each one as a potential king, the Lord cautioned him, "Do not look at his appearance or at the height of his stature, because I have refused him. For the Lord does not see as man sees; for man looks at the outward appearance, but the Lord looks at the heart" (I Sam. 16:7 NKJV). After looking over seven of Jesse's sons, the prophet said flatly, "The Lord has not chosen these." Then he asked, "Are these all the children?" Jesse had not even thought of his youngest as a candidate. "There remains yet the youngest, and behold, he is tending the sheep." Samuel asked that David be brought to him.

The description of the young shepherd brought before Samuel underlines the outward manifestation of his heart.

"Now he was ruddy, with beautiful eyes and a handsome appearance." As Samuel studied David's face, the Lord spoke the undeniable command of his choice. "Arise, anoint him; for this is he." And so, the elderly prophet took his horn of oil and anointed David while his astonished brothers and father looked on in amazement. The Spirit of the Lord came mightily upon David from that day forward. God entrusted his heart to the receptive and ready heart of David.

God is seeking to find that quality of heart in you and me. In every period of history, circumstance, or time of personal or interpersonal crisis, he searches for a person whose heart wants his heart. The significant thing about David's call is that he did not think of himself as a future leader of Israel who would need God's help to accomplish his self-image of greatness. He longed for God's heart and God did the rest. When we put God first in our lives, he can use us. We do not seek God to accomplish our ends. We love God for God, not for what he can do for us. Our analysis of what he could do through us usually hits wide of the mark. An authentic call always has in it a surprise and a mystery. We are responsible only for what is in our hearts. Our minds, emotions, and will. Begin there and leave the results to him!

Lloyd J. Ogilvie

"Don't forget," admonished Peter, "that we couldn't understand why he wanted to leave Canaan and come to Capernaum."

"That was different," mumbled Thomas. "He felt that he was urgently needed there." "Maybe he feels that he is now needed elsewhere," observed Andrew, to which James added, "I don't believe he cares very much whether we understand him or not."

"You are right, Jimmy," rumbled old Bartholomew. "He's teaching us to have faith in him."

"But—can't a man have faith—and understanding, too?" argued Thomas.

"No!" declared Bartholomew, bluntly. "That's what faith is for, my son! It's for when we can't understand!"

"That's true!" approved Peter. "When a man understands, he doesn't need any faith."

"I don't like to be kept in the dark," put in Philip.

"If a man has enough faith," replied Peter, "he can find his way in the dark—with faith as his lamp."

Lloyd C. Douglas
(from *The Big Fisherman*)

THE GIFT OF FAITH

We live in a maze of symbols, all of them from the sun to a bird's feather, from the Bach B minor Mass down to the echo of a bell, uniting to give us this multi-coloured treasure that starts us off on the journey that has been described down the centuries in so many myths and stories, but is always the same journey. The prodigal son and the Magi were journeying to the same place and Person; they were hunters on the same trail. The prodigal son caught the scent of some remembered goodness, the fragrance of some garden at life's beginning and of Someone who had walked with him there. Or so, on his good days, the song of the birds and the colours of the wayside flowers seemed to tell him. . . . On his bad days he could not smell a thing; except the stink of his own dirt. . . . But he went on, sometimes with the faint sound of water in his ears from far-off streams. How could he know that at the other end of the trail another hunter was running out to meet him? And how could the Magi know either in those times of darkness and confusion that when their star blinked and went out, and they floundered off the road, they would ever get on it again? It was only when the stable door opened and the light came down the path to meet them that they knew their journey had not been hopeless.

The author of the Epiphany collect must have been much like Saint Paul, for he speaks with the same shattering confidence. "Mercifully grant that we, which know thee now by faith, may after this life have the fruition of thy glorious God-head." The fruition, the completeness of the Godhead. What a thing to dare to hope for! It sounds ridiculous, yet both men, and an amazing number of saints and mystics both before and after them, have said the same thing. . . . We exhausted, futile travellers, losing the way, falling in the dark, struggling on again, will ultimately get there. . . . It is an immense hope and is the gift of faith.

Elizabeth Goudge

FREEDOM

. . . He looked down for a moment and touched the book of poetry. "I believe I have the answer to Blake's question, 'What can this Gospel of Jesus be?' It's freedom, dear Charlotte—freedom from the past and hope for the future, for eternity, because of our Lord's sacrifice."

He stopped talking, his eyes brightening with unshed tears, and looked toward the view of the sea—the waves crashing forever mercilessly against the unrelenting cliffs. "Do you like John Donne?" he asked. Then, quietly, he recited:

> Batter my heart, three personed God; for you
> As yet but knock, breathe, shine, and seek to mend. . . .
> I like a usurped town, to another due,
> Labor to admit you, but, oh, to no end.

In a quiet, yet strong voice, he said, "Like Donne, I asked God to 'batter my heart.' And . . . finally . . . I willingly admitted Him . . ."

Joan Winmill Brown
(from *Penross Manor*)

Here is the wisdom of the contented man:
to let God choose for him;
for when we have given up our wills to Him . . .
our spirits must needs rest while our conditions
have for their security the power,
the wisdom, and the charity of God.

Bishop Jeremy Taylor
1613–1667

What can I give Him
Poor as I am?
If I were a shepherd,
I would give a lamb.
If I were a Wise Man,
I would do my part,—
But what I can I give Him,
Give my heart.

Christina G. Rossetti
1830–1894

These two entries in Queen Victoria's diary—written a year apart, during her annual stay in Scotland—illustrate her openness to worship and to learn more of our Lord:

THE KIRK (THE CHURCH)

October 29, 1854

We went to Kirk, as usual, at twelve o'clock. The service was performed by the Rev. Norman McLeod, of *Glasgow*, son of Dr. McLeod, and any thing finer I never heard. The sermon, entirely extempore, was quite admirable; so simple, and yet so eloquent, and so beautifully argued and put. The text was from the account of the coming of Nicodemus to Christ by night; St. John, chapter iii. Mr. McLeod showed in the sermon how we *all* tried to please *self*, and live for *that*, and in so doing found no rest. Christ had come not only to die for us, but to show how we were to live. The second prayer was very touching; his allusions to us were so simple, saying, after his mention of us, "bless their children." It gave me a lump in my throat, as also when he prayed for "the dying, the wounded, the widow, and the orphans." Every one came back delighted; and how satisfactory it is to come back from church with such feelings! The servants and the Highlanders—*all*— were equally delighted.

October 14, 1855

To Kirk at twelve o'clock. The Rev. J. Caird, one of the most celebrated preachers in *Scotland*, performed the service, and electrified all present by a most admirable and beautiful sermon, which lasted nearly an hour, but which kept one's attention riveted. The text was from the twelfth chapter of Romans, and the eleventh verse: *"Not slothful in business; fervent in spirit; serving the Lord."* He explained, in the most beautiful and simple manner, what real religion is; how it ought to pervade every action of our lives; not a thing only for Sundays, or for our closet; not a thing to drive us from the world; not "perpetual moping over 'good' books," but "being and doing good"; "letting every thing be done in a Christian spirit." It was as fine as Mr. McLeod's sermon last year, and sent us home much edified.

Queen Victoria

We praise thee, we bless thee, we worship thee, we glorify thee, we give thanks to thee for thy great glory, O Lord God, heavenly King, God the Father Almighty.

Book of Common Prayer

"Praise My Soul, the King of Heaven," is a paraphrase of Psalm 103, and is a favorite of Queen Elizabeth II. This hymn was sung at her coronation:

> Praise my soul, the King of Heaven,
> To His feet thy tribute bring;
> Ransomed, healed, restored, forgiven,
> Who like me, His praise should sing?
> Alleluia, Alleluia,
> Praise the everlasting King!

Henry F. Lyte

4

Our love for Him leads us to service.

Use me, God, in Thy great harvest field,
Which stretcheth far and wide like a wide sea;
The gatherers are so few; I fear the precious yield
Will suffer loss. Oh, find a place for me!
A place where best the strength I have will tell;
It may be one the older toilers shun;
Be it a wide or narrow place, 'tis well
So that the work it holds be only done.

Christina G. Rossetti
1830–1894

WHAT IS HIS WILL?

It seems to me we need to ask more seriously than in by-gone days, what is really the will and command of our blessed Lord? and to set about obeying Him, not merely in attempting to obey. I do not know that we are told anywhere in the Bible to try to do anything. "We must try to do the best we can," is a very common expression; but I remember some years ago, after a remark of that kind, looking very carefully through the New Testament to see under what circumstances the disciples were told to try to do anything. I was surprised that I did not find any instance. Then I went through the Old Testament with the same result. There are many commands apparently impossible to obey, but they were all definite commands.

God gives His spirit, not to those who long for Him, not to those who pray for Him, not to those who desire to be filled always; but He does give His Holy Spirit to them that obey Him.

Hudson Taylor

O Savior pour upon me thy Spirit of meekness and love! Annihilate the Selfhood in me: be thou my life!

William Blake
1757–1827
(from "Jerusalem 'Invocation'")

Once I rode out into the woods for my health. Having alighted from my horse in a retired place as my manner commonly had been, to walk for divine contemplation and prayer, I had a view—that was for me extraordinary—of the glory of the Son of God. As near as I can judge, this continued about

70

an hour; and kept me the greater part of the time in a flood of tears and weeping aloud. I felt an ardency of soul to be—what I know not otherwise how to express—*emptied and annihilated; to love Him with a holy and pure love; to serve and follow Him; to be perfectly sanctified, and made pure with a divine and heavenly purity.*

Jonathan Edwards
1703–1758

Almighty One, in the woods I am blessed. Happy everyone in the woods. Every tree speaks through thee. O God! What glory in the woodland! On the heights is peace—peace to serve Him.

Ludwig van Beethoven
1770–1827

A SURRENDER OF SELF

Until you have given up your self to Him you will not have a real self. Sameness is to be found most among the most "natural" men, not among those who surrender to Christ. How monotonously alike all the great tyrants and conquerors have been: how gloriously different are the saints.

But there must be a real giving up of the self. You must throw it away "blindly" so to speak. Christ will indeed give you a real personality: but you must not go to Him for the sake of that. As long as your own personality is what you are bothering about you are not going to Him at all. The very first step is to try to forget about the self altogether. Your real, new self (which is Christ's and also yours, and yours just because it is His) will not come as long as you are looking for it. It will come when you are looking for Him. Does that sound strange? The same principle holds, you know, for more everyday matters. Even in social life, you will never make a good impression on other people until you stop thinking

71

about what sort of impression you are making. Even in literature and art, no man who bothers about originality will ever be original: whereas if you simply try to tell the truth (without caring twopence how often it has been told before) you will, nine times out of ten, become original without ever having noticed it. The principle runs through all life from top to bottom. Give up yourself, and you will find your real self. Lose your life and you will save it. Submit to death, death of your ambitions and favourite wishes every day and death of your whole body in the end: submit with every fibre of your being, and you will find eternal life. Keep back nothing. Nothing that you have not given away will ever be really yours. Nothing in you that has not died will ever be raised from the dead. Look for yourself, and you will find in the long run only hatred, loneliness, despair, rage, ruin, and decay. But look for Christ and you will find Him, and with Him everything else thrown in.

C. S. Lewis

What is Christian perfection? Loving God with all our heart, mind, soul and strength.

John Wesley
1703–1791

FROM "WHERE LOVE IS, THERE GOD IS ALSO"

. . . Martin buried the little fellow and was inconsolable. Indeed, he was so inconsolable that he began to murmur against God. His life seemed so empty that more than once he prayed for death and reproached the Almighty for taking away his only beloved son instead of himself, the old man. At last he ceased altogether to go to church.

Then one day there came to see him an ancient peasant-pilgrim—one who was now in the eighth year of his pilgrimage. To him Avdeitch talked, and then went on to complain of his great sorrow.

"I no longer wish to be a God-fearing man," he said. "I only wish to die. That is all I ask of God. I am a lonely, hopeless man."

"You should not speak like that, Martin," replied the old pilgrim. "It is not for us to judge the acts of God. We must rely, not upon our own understanding, but upon the Divine wisdom. God saw fit that your son should die and that you should live. Therefore it must be better so. If you despair, it is because you have wished to live too much for your own pleasure."

"For what, then, should I live?" asked Martin.

"For God alone," replied the old man. "It is He who gave you life, and therefore it is He for whom you should live. When you come to live for Him you will cease to grieve, and your trials will become easy to bear."

Martin was silent. Then he spoke again.

"But how am I to live for God?" he asked.

"Christ has shown us the way," answered the old man. "Can you read? If so, buy a Testament and study it. You will learn there how to live for God. Yes, it is all shown there."

These words sank into Avdeitch's soul. He went out the same day, bought a large-print copy of the New Testament, and set himself to read it.

At the beginning Avdeitch had meant only to read on festival days, but when he once began his reading he found it so comforting to the soul that he came never to let a day pass without doing so. On the second occasion he became so engrossed that all the kerosene was burnt away in the lamp before he could tear himself away from the book.

Thus he came to read it every evening, and, the more he read, the more clearly did he understand what God required of him, and in what way he could live for God; so that his heart grew ever lighter and lighter. Once upon a time, whenever he had lain down to sleep, he had been used to moan and sigh as he thought of his little Kapitoshka; but now he only said— "Glory to Thee, O Lord! Glory to Thee! Thy will be done!"

Count Leo Tolstoy
1828–1910

Keep us, Lord, so awake in the duties of our calling that we may sleep in thy peace and wake in thy glory.

John Donne
1572–1631

A distant cousin of Elizabeth Barrett Browning wrote her suggesting that references to her belief in Christianity might hurt the sales of her poetry. Here is what she replied:

Certainly I would rather be a pagan whose religion was actual, earnest, continual—than I would be a Christian who, from whatever motive, shrank from hearing or uttering the name of Christ out of a "church." I am no fanatic, but I like truth and earnestness in all things, and I cannot choose but that such a Christian shows but ill beside such a pagan. What pagan poet ever thought of casting his gods out of his poetry?. . .And if I shrank from naming the name of my God lest it should not meet the sympathy of some readers, or lest it should offend the delicacies of other readers, or lest, generally, it should be unfit for the purposes of poetry, in what more forcible manner than by that act can I secure to myself unanswerable shame?

Elizabeth Barrett Browning
1806–1861

To become Christlike is the only thing in the whole world worth caring for, the thing before which every ambition of man is folly and all lower achievement vain.

Henry Drummond
1851–1897

The maturity of a Christian experience cannot be reached in a moment, but is the result of the work of God's Holy Spirit, who, by His energizing and transforming power, causes us to grow up into Christ in all things. And we cannot hope to reach this maturity in any way other than by yielding ourselves up, utterly and willingly, to His mighty working. But the sanctification the Scriptures urge, as a present experience upon all believers, does not consist in maturity of growth, but in purity of heart; and this may be as complete in the early as in our later experiences.

The lump of clay, from the moment it comes under the transforming hand of the potter is, during each day and each hour of the process, just what the potter wants it to be at that hour or on that day, and therefore pleases him; but it is very far from being matured into the vessel he intends in the future to make it.

The little babe may be all that a babe could be, or ought to be, and may therefore perfectly please its mother; and yet it is very far from being what that mother would wish it to be when the years of maturity shall come.

The apple in June is a perfect apple for June; it is the best apple that June can produce: but it is very different from the apple in October, which is a perfected apple.

God's works are perfect in every stage of their growth. Man's works are never perfect until they are in every respect complete.

Hannah Whitall Smith

God hasn't given up yet on His world, which is one world, and could be one world of security, peace and brotherhood instead of two worlds of suspicion and fear.

God hasn't given up on this country, which is His latest experiment in human freedom and opportunity.

God hasn't given up on you.

He can still do great things for you, in you, and through you.

God is ready and waiting and able.

What about you, and me?

We are, after all, like lumps of clay.

There are brittle pieces, hard pieces.

We have little shape or beauty.

But we need not despair.

If we are clay, let us remember there is a Potter, and His wheel.

The old gospel song has it right:

> Have Thine own way, Lord,
> Have Thine own way.
> Thou art the Potter, I am the clay;
> Mould me and make me, after Thy will,
> While I am waiting, yielded and still.
>
> *[Adelaide T. Pollard]*

That's it.

We have only to be yielded, that is, willing, surrendered, and He will do the rest.

He will make us according to the pattern for which, in His love, He designed us.

And it will be good—for our own good—and for His glory.

Do not despair.

If you want to be different, you may.

You, too, can be changed for the better. Therein lies our hope—and the hope of the world.

We are disciples in clay.

And there is still the skill of the Potter.

Peter Marshall

RECKLESS DEVOTION

Apostolic Christianity was distinguished by a wholehearted, reckless devotion to Jesus Christ. He was the center on which the lives of those early Christians revolved. They did

not understand him—they could not explain him to themselves, not to mention outsiders, but they trusted him, loved
him and obeyed him. They were far from perfect in their lives,
but there was a kind of abandoned unselfconsciousness about
them. If they were preoccupied, it was with the matchless One
who had mastered them, possessed them, and for whom they
would gladly lay down their lives. This is the Christianity of the
New Testament: commitment to a Person!

Richard C. Halverson
(Chaplain of the United States Senate)

With infinite care and forethought God has chosen the best
place in which you can do your best work for the world. You
may be lonely, but you have no more right to complain than
the lamp has, which has been placed in a niche to illumine a
dark landing or a flight of dangerous stone steps. The master
of the house may have put you in a very small corner and on a
very humble stand; but it is enough if it be His blessed will.
Some day He will pass by, and you shall light His steps as He
goes forth to seek and save that which is lost; or you shall
kindle some great light that shall shine like a beacon over the
storm-swept ocean. Thus the obscure Andrew was the means
of igniting his brother Peter, when he brought him to Jesus.

Selected

We meet sordidness, ugliness and drabness not with the
defense of hardening ourselves so that we cannot see or feel it,
but by meeting it squarely, recognizing it and then looking
through it to the glory and the beauty that lie beyond and
beneath it. A life that has not glory in it is not beautiful; a soul
that has not vision is surely dead; but in almost every life,
even of those who have never heard the Gospel, one can
glimpse beauty, wistfulness, hunger for better things, if one
looks well. It is called "second sight"—to see the souls of men,
not just their clothes, to see "The Common Street" lit up with
heaven's glory.

And yet, from sordid and from base,
Passion can lift a shining face . . .
And walking through a street at night
I saw a jail in soft moonlight;
And there, behind the chequered bars,
A still shape came to look at stars . . .
                                        Conrad Aiken

To those who hunger—"the Bread of Life" . . . To those
who thirst—"the Living Water" . . . To those who come "to
look at stars"—the beauty of the message of God, of love,
peace through Christ, truth and everlasting sureties . . .
Who would not be willing to stand in the market place to tell
this message to the common people of the world?
"And the common people heard him *gladly.*"

Lillian Dickson

LORD, MAKE ME GENEROUS

Several years ago, Mother Teresa of Calcutta came to
Washington to share her deep faith and tell us about her work
among the dying and homeless of India. Louie and I were
privileged to be among the guests at a small luncheon in her
honor in the office of a mutual friend in the Senate. I wish I
could find words to describe the effect Mother Teresa had on
my life that day. I can't. Neither can Louie, for after the
luncheon and a meeting that night at National Presbyterian
Church, where this remarkable woman spoke to people from
all over the city, my husband turned to me—his arms out-
stretched and his eyes brimming—and said: "What do we do
with a person like this?"

Everything about Mother Teresa was so simple: her muslin
habit—fastened with a safety pin—her face, her gaze, and
especially her words. Even now, her answers to questions
asked of her that day ring in my heart as models of gospel
clarity and truth. When our host, the senator, a caring and
sensitive Christian, asked Mother Teresa how she dealt with

the lack of success in her work because such a high percentage of those she sought to help died in her arms, her answer was: "Jesus hasn't called me to be successful. Only faithful."

Those words have had a powerful influence in my life. When I hear about the overwhelming needs in our world—when I see some of them right outside my front door—the small efforts I make through a hunger committee, through an adopt-a-block program, through a covenant with the poor, seem desperately insignificant.

But then I remind myself that while I can never eradicate such a need, I can be faithful to what God asks of me day by day. And I thank Him and His servant Teresa.

A *Living Bible* is open on my desk, and my eyes just fell on 2 Corinthians 9:8, 9: "God is able to make it up to you by giving you everything you need and more, so that there will not only be enough for your own needs, but plenty left over to give joyfully to others. . . . the godly man gives generously to the poor. . . ."

Colleen Townsend Evans

HALLOWED BE THY NAME

There are hungry hearts who will never realize their need because they do not know what it is they desire until one day they see the Lord Jesus in you. It is that incarnate revelation of Jesus Christ in the life of a Christian which makes men and women thirst after God, for it crystallizes the thing that they have been seeking and cannot express. It meets the need of the heart which is burdened and lonely and troubled and does not know the answer. The moment they see a child of God who hallows the name of God, at that moment they see one who possesses what they need. Oh, that His name might be hallowed, that Father-relationship honored, that Christ-image recognized, so that the very life you and I live in ordinary surroundings may be so clear and transparent that it will bring others face to face with reality!

Alan Redpath

Fill Thou my life, O Lord my God,
  In every part with praise,
That my whole being may proclaim
  Thy being and Thy ways.
Not for the lip of praise alone,
  Nor e'en the praising heart
I ask, but for a life made up
  Of praise in every part.

So shall each fear, each fret, each care
  Be turned into a song,
And every winding of the way
  The echo shall prolong:

So shall no part of day or night
  From sacredness be free:
But all my life, in every step,
  Be fellowship with Thee.

Horatio Bonar

If I could give you information of my life it would be to
show how a woman of very ordinary ability has been led by
God in strange and unaccustomed paths to do in His service
what He has done in her. And if I could tell you all, you
would see how God has done all, and I nothing. I have
worked hard, very hard, that is all; and I have never refused
God anything.

Florence Nightingale
1820–1910

LIVING LIFE AS A PRIVILEGE

Looking at life as a privilege produces a radical change in us; I learned that secret from James Stewart one summer years ago. He had been one of my professors during my student days at New College in Edinburgh, Scotland. Through the years in the ministry, refresher courses and visits with Dr. Stewart have enriched my life immeasurably. During one of those visits, I confessed my battle with time and the exhaustion I was feeling after a busy year of ministry. His advice was liberating. "Lloyd, do what you can in any day. Expect the Lord to intervene with supernatural power, and live life as a privilege!"

From that advice I adopted a three-word model. I say it to myself at the beginning of each day and all through the pressures of the day. It's become my life slogan. "It's a privilege!"

I've discovered that by repeating those three words all through the day, I can transform the dull routines as well as the exciting opportunities into Christ-events. That includes everything from the mundane duties of life and a desk piled high with things to do, to meeting with people and to preaching the Gospel. It's a privilege to be alive, to be filled with Christ's Spirit, to see what He's going to do with the challenges in my life.

Lloyd J. Ogilvie

O Lord God, we pray that we may be inspired to nobleness of life in the least things. May we dignify all our daily life. May we set such a sacredness upon every part of our life, that nothing shall be trivial, nothing unimportant, and nothing dull, in the daily round. Amen.

Henry Ward Beecher
1813–1837

FINDING GOD IN OUR WORK

God does not deflect our gaze prematurely from the work He Himself has given us, since He presents Himself to us as attainable through that very work. Nor does He blot out, in His intense light, the detail of our earthly aims, since the closeness of our union with Him is in fact determined by the exact fulfilment of the least of our tasks. . . . God, in all that is most living and incarnate in Him, is not far away from us, altogether apart from the world we see, touch, hear, smell and taste about us. Rather He awaits us every instant in our action, in the work of the moment. There is a sense in which He is at the tip of my pen, my spade, my brush, my needle— of my heart and of my thought. By pressing the stroke, the line, or the stitch, on which I am engaged, to its ultimate natural finish, I shall lay hold of the last end towards which my innermost will tends. . . . Try, with God's help, to per- ceive the connection—even physical and natural—which binds your labour with the building of the Kingdom of Heaven; try to realise that heaven itself smiles upon you and, through your works, draws you to itself; then, as you leave church for the noisy streets, you will remain with only one feeling, that of continuing to immerse yourself in God. . . . Never, at any time . . . consent to do anything without first of all realising its significance and constructive value in Christo Jesu, and pursuing it with all your might. This is not simply a commonplace precept for salvation: it is the very path to sanctity for each man according to his state and calling. For what is sanctity in a creature if not to adhere to God with the maximum of his strength?—and what does that maximum adherence to God mean if not the fulfilment—in the world organised around Christ—of the exact function, be it lowly or eminent, to which that creature is destined both by natural endowment and by supernatural gift?

Pierre Teilhard de Chardin
(from *Le Milieu Divin*)

I HAVE A NEED

"I have a need." How many times a day do you hear it as you help your family and friends over the bumps of life? Is your telephone ringing throughout the daylight hours to let you know your vote is needed—or your service, presence, donation? Even the inanimate objects in my house seem to have voices: "Fix us . . . find us . . . turn us on . . . off . . . clean us . . . fill us up!" Do any of these, living or non-living, know of *my* needs?

I need to be alone. I need time . . . I need—but why go on? Need is a common denominator of our lives, isn't it? Many of the needs can be filled with loving arms of family, understanding of friends, services of our hairdressers, doctors, lawyers, florists and butchers. But there's a greater need: I need Christ—a great Christ; and I have a great Christ to fill my need. How futile all these other things would seem without Him to lead me, guide me, keep me on course. The mind's-eye of my mortal being is so short-sighted, it's difficult for me to envision the greatness of His power, even when I acknowledge that without Him I can do nothing. Can you think of One who controls things: the ability to heal the sick, bring joy to the lonely, rest to the weary, new life to the dead; and yet has need of us? Too often I forget that Jesus, who is all confidence, power, commitment, love and the giver of the Kingdom of Heaven, still needs me to carry on in my own way to spread His message—by word, maybe; by deed, probably; by example, *always*.

When we think, "I have a great need; I have a Great Christ for that need. Christ has a need of my service," then small frustrations of the day become nothing. And while the big ones may stick around to discourage, frustrate and disappoint us, we find that we can bear them.

June Masters Bacher

DEAR LORD AND FATHER OF MANKIND

Dear Lord and Father of mankind!
  Forgive our foolish ways!
Reclothe us in our rightful mind,
In purer lives Thy service find,
  In deeper reverence, praise.

In simple trust like theirs who heard,
  Beside the Syrian sea,
The gracious calling of the Lord,
Let us, like them, without a word,
  Rise up and follow Thee.

O Sabbath rest by Galilee!
  O calm of hills above,
Where Jesus knelt to share with Thee
The silence of eternity
  Interpreted by love!

With that deep hush subduing all
  Our words and works that drown
The tender whisper of Thy call,
As noiseless let Thy blessing fall
  As fell Thy manna down.

Drop Thy still dews of quietness,
  Till all our strivings cease;
Take from our souls the strain and stress,
And let our ordered lives confess
  The beauty of Thy peace.

Breathe through the heats of our desire
  Thy coolness and Thy balm;
Let sense be dumb, let flesh retire;
Speak through the earthquake, wind and fire,
  O still small voice of calm!

John Greenleaf Whittier
1807–1892

84

A SENSE OF CONFIDENCE IN THE
RESULTS OF GOD'S WORK

The marvel and mystery of God's ways in his life had our psalmist wide-eyed with amazement. He had *full confidence in God's sovereign power:* "I praise thee, for thou art fearful and wonderful. Wonderful are thy works!" (Psalm 139:14). And why not such praise? If God can fashion unique human persons capable of loving him and serving others from a couple of dots of living tissue, what can he not do? A knowledge of the many and varied facets of his providence sets us free to trust him, to believe that he will work—even through us.

The psalmist also had *full confidence in God's personal knowledge:* "How precious to me are thy thoughts, O God! How vast is the sum of them!" (Psalm 139:17). And why not such exclamation? God knows the plan of our days before they ever happen. When we did not have him in mind at all, he was already cherishing us and reserving for us a place in his plan. That is thoughtfulness at its highest. Small wonder that we can count on him to carry out his mission—and to use us in it.

Doubt, discouragement, self-depreciation—these are worldly, not biblical, attitudes. We can always wish we were different or better. And there is ample room for improvement among even the best of God's people. But we must not disparage God's handiwork. That remarkable set of natural and spiritual abilities that combine in us are his doing. And he does all things well.

David Allan Hubbard

A GRACIOUS INVITATION

I think at this juncture in my life I am becoming more and more aware that I am not smart enough to make all the decisions I must make. Neither am I strong enough to do all the things I should be doing. I'm not nearly wise enough to properly choose the path through the myriad ways that life can go wrong. So it comes as deep consolation and comfort to me to know that if I will begin right, if I will live in the Spirit, if I will seek to be like him, he will see to the endings.

What a calling it is! A calling to be finished and done with impurity, greed, hatred, jealousy, selfish ambition, and envy— to name a few of the things Paul lists as marks of being "like them." His call to love, joy, peace, patience, kindness, goodness, faithfulness, gentleness, and self-control.

Have you ever felt you should be true? Have you ever been impressed to be faithful? Have you known you should be honest? Have you ever wanted to know joy? Have you ever desired goodness, or wanted to live in peace? Have you ever wished that you were loving, and patient, and kind?

Then you have heard his voice. From deep within, he was calling you to be free.

Bob Benson

Make a joyful noise unto the Lord, all ye lands.
    Serve the Lord with gladness:
    come before his presence with singing.
Know ye that the Lord he is God:
    it is he that hath made us, and not we ourselves;
    we are his people, and the sheep of his pasture.
Enter into his gates with thanksgiving,
    and into his courts with praise:
    be thankful unto him, and bless his name.
For the Lord is good;
    his mercy is everlasting;
    and his truth endureth to all generations.

Psalm 100

At the moment of His Ascension,
    when the Apostles watched Jesus rise before them,
    perfectly naturally
    and with every right,
  they grew aware—
    for the first time, no doubt—
    of their mysterious companion's true identity.

They started to understand
　　who Jesus was,
　　what He'd done for them
　　and how they'd received Him.
　　For three years
　　　God had lived with them,
　　　God had eaten at their table,
　　　God had slept in their homes,
　　　God had told them all about Himself—
　　　and they'd never even thanked Him.
Now they saw how rude and thoughtless they'd been;
　　they saw everything they could've done for Him,
　　　everything they could've said,
　　　all the happiness they could've given Him.
"And they stood there, gazing up in to heaven."
　　Heaven'd begun thirty-three years before,
　　and they hadn't noticed.

But angels came to shake them,
　　　rouse them from their nostalgia
　　　and send them into the world,
　　　　where their Master was waiting
　　　　for them.
It wasn't too late, they realized.
　　Now they could do for men
　　　all they were sorry they hadn't done for Christ.
　　Together, they'd renew the great Adventure
　　　that'd never end.
They were going to live heaven on earth.

Louis Evely
(translated by Edmond Bonin)

GOD'S DIVINE LESSONS

The life of a Christian is an education for higher service. No athlete complains when the training is hard. He thinks of the game, or the race. As the Apostle Paul wrote:

In my opinion, whatever we may have to go through now is less than nothing compared with the magnificent future God has planned for us. The whole creation is on tiptoe to see the wonderful sight of the sons of God coming into their own. The world of creation cannot as yet see reality, not because it chooses to be blind, but because in God's purpose it has been so limited—yet it has been given hope. And the hope is that in the end the whole of created life will be rescued from the tryanny of change and decay and have its share in that magnificent liberty which can only belong to the children of God!

It is plain to anyone with eyes to see that at present time all created life groans in a sort of universal travail. And it is plain, too, that we who have a foretaste of the Spirit are in a state of painful tension, while we wait for that redemption of our bodies which will mean that at last we have realized our full sonship in him (Romans 8:18–23, PHILLIPS).

Looking back across the years of my life, I can see the working of a divine pattern which is the way of God with His children. When I was in a prison camp in Holland during the war, I often prayed, "Lord, never let the enemy put me in a German concentration camp." God answered *no* to that prayer. Yet in the German camp, with all its horror, I found many prisoners who had never heard of Jesus Christ. If God had not used my sister Betsie and me to bring them to Him, they would never have heard of Him. Many died, or were killed, but many died with the Name of Jesus on their lips. They were well worth all our suffering. Faith is like radar which sees through the fog—the reality of things at a distance that the human eye cannot see.

My life is but a weaving, between my God and me,
I do not choose the colors, He worketh steadily,
Oftimes He weaveth sorrow, and I in foolish pride,
Forget He sees the upper, and I the underside.
Not till the loom is silent, and shuttles cease to fly,
Will God unroll the canvas and explain the reason why.
The dark threads are as needful in the skillful Weaver's hand,
As the threads of gold and silver in the pattern He has planned.

Anonymous

Although the threads of my life have often seemed knotted, I know, by faith, that on the other side of the embroidery there is a crown. As I have walked the world—a tramp for the Lord—I have learned a few lessons in God's great classroom. . . . I pray the Holy Spirit will reveal something of the divine pattern in God's plan for you also.

Corrie Ten Boom

O Give thanks unto the Lord, sing unto Him; sing praises unto Him, for the precious things of heaven, for the dew, and for the deep that crouches beneath, and for the precious fruits brought forth from the sun, and for the precious things put forth by the moon, and for the chief things of the ancient mountains, and for the precious things of the everlasting hills, and for the precious things of the earth, and its fullness. Let everything that has breath praise the Lord. Praise ye the Lord.

Governor William Bradford

Part Three

My Heart Sings

5

Nothing can separate us from the joy that comes in knowing we are loved by God.

How soon a smile of God can change the world!
How we are made for happiness—how work
Grows play, adversity a winning fight!

Robert Browning
1812–1889

Joy is prayer—Joy is strength—Joy is love—Joy is a net of love by which you can catch souls. She gives most who gives with joy.

The best way to show our gratitude to God and the people is to accept everything with joy. A joyful heart is the inevitable result of a heart burning with love.

We all long for heaven where God is but we have it in our power to be in heaven with Him right now—to be happy with Him at this very moment. But being happy with Him now means:

loving as He loves,
helping as he helps,
giving as He gives,
serving as He serves,
rescuing as He rescues,
being with Him for all the twenty-four hours,
touching Him in His distressing disguise.

Mother Teresa

HE LOVED LIFE

"In Him was *life*," says St. John. He was made for life. He loved life passionately. We do not honour Jesus by imagining that He accepted Calvary easily. He hated death. Death was one of the powers He had come to destroy. But to Jesus, God's will was everything. It was God's will that the world should be redeemed; and if the achievement of that redemption lay on the road of the supreme sacrifice, then—welcome Death! That was Jesus' spirit. He loved life dearly, but He loved God's will far more. And mingling with the ecstasy of the Transfiguration was the joy of an absolute self-consecration, a divine joy whose light in that moment flooded His soul and shone out on His face, and brought His amazed disciples down in adoration at His feet.

Hence from the heart of this mysterious crisis in the life of Jesus, a clear challenge reaches us all. The one thing for which we have been created is the doing of the will of God. Obedience to that will may mean sacrifice, and self-negation, and the hard road of the Cross; but there alone can joy be found, and peace, and a life made radiant and shining like the sun. The road of self-consecration is the King's highway; and we are lost if we are not travelling there.

James S. Stewart

Thou wilt show me the path of life:
   in thy presence is fulness of joy;
   at thy right hand there are pleasures for evermore.

Psalm 16:11

The theme of love permeates the Bible. In the Song of Solomon, that beautiful canticle of love, the bridegroom sings, "Set me as a seal upon thine heart, as a seal upon thine arm: for love is strong as death . . ." (Song of Sol. 8:6).

A very clear picture of love's compelling power is given in the book of Hebrews: "Looking unto Jesus the author and finisher of our faith; who for the joy that was set before him endured the cross, despising the shame, and is set down at the right hand of the throne of God" (12:2). What is the joy that was set before Jesus? What did he have after his ascension that he did not have before he took on human flesh? Us . . . you and me . . . the redemption of all mankind. Is this not love?

God loved us so much, he gave his Son, and ever since that first advent love has been defined in terms of giving. What more could Jesus have done to convince us of his overwhelming love? Nothing! The Cross was the ultimate evidence.

Under the shower of God's love for us as individuals, love ceases to be just something we feel; it is something we share. A life yielded to Christ can see love's power bring transfor-

95

mation. And then it will spill over on to others. Amy Carmichael summed it up when she said, "You can give without loving but you can't love without giving."

Twila Knaack

Isa. 35.7 (LXX): There shall there be a joy of birds.

Ps. 50.1 (LXX): I know all the birds of the sky.

The joy of birds is one of the most wonderful things about them. They seem to sing the moment they awake, even if they are wakened by cold wind and rain. They sing before they set to work to find something to eat. And not one is forgotten by God who knows all the birds of the sky.

Not one of us is forgotten, either; not one of us is overlooked. Not a song we sing is forgotten or overlooked. The God of the joy of the birds wants our joy too.

Some of us cannot sing beautiful songs. Many birds cannot. There is one who can only sing "Pretty dear," and another who only sings "Be quick." But not a bird says, "My song is too small to be worth singing." And He who loves the joy of birds listens.

Because He knows all the birds of the sky He would know if there was one who would not sing, and He would miss that song. Is there one of us whose song He is missing today?

Amy Carmichael

SURPRISED BY JOY

I had always wanted, above all things, not to be "interfered with." I had wanted (mad wish) "to call my soul my own." I had been far more anxious to avoid suffering than to achieve delight. I had always aimed at limited liabilities. The supernatural itself had been to me, first, an illicit dram, and then, as by a drunkard's reaction, nauseous. Even my recent attempt to live my philosophy had secretly (I now knew) been hedged round by all sorts of reservations. I had pretty well known that my ideal of virtue would never be allowed to lead me into anything intolerably painful; I would be "reasonable." But now what had been an ideal became a command; and what might not be expected of one? Doubtless, by definition, God was Reason itself. But would He also be "reasonable" in that other, more comfortable, sense? Not the slightest assurance on that score was offered me. Total surrender, the absolute leap in the dark, were demanded. The reality with which no treaty can be made was upon me. The demand was not even "All or nothing." I think that stage had been passed, on the bus top when I unbuckled my armor and the snowman started to melt. Now, the demand was simply "All."

You must picture me alone in that room in Magdalen, night after night, feeling, whenever my mind lifted even for a second from my work, the steady, unrelenting approach of Him whom I so earnestly desired not to meet. That which I greatly feared had at last come upon me. In the Trinity Term of 1929 I gave in, and admitted that God was God, and knelt and prayed: perhaps, that night, the most dejected and reluctant convert in all England. I did not then see what is now the most shining and obvious thing; the Divine humility which will accept a convert even on such terms. The Prodigal Son at least walked home on his own feet. But who can duly adore that Love which will open the high gates to a prodigal who is brought in kicking, struggling, resentful, and darting his eyes in every direction for a chance of escape? The words *compelle intrare*, compel them to come in, have been so abused by wicked men that we shudder at them; but, properly understood, they plumb the depth of the Divine mercy. The hardness of God is kinder than the softness of men, and His compulsion is our liberation.

C. S. Lewis

Let us then think only of the present, and not permit our minds to wander with curiosity into the future. This future is not yet ours; perhaps it never will be. It is exposing ourselves to temptation to wish to anticipate God, and to prepare ourselves for things which he may not destine for us. If such things should come to pass, he will give us light and strength according to the need. Why should we desire to meet difficulties prematurely, when we have neither strength nor light as yet provided for them? Let us give heed to the present, whose duties are pressing; it is fidelity to the present which prepares us for fidelity in the future.

Francois Fénelon

God has many ways of drawing us to Himself, He sometimes hides Himself from us; but faith alone, which will not fail us in time of need, ought to be our support, and the foundation of our confidence, which must be all in God.

I know not how God will dispose of me. I am always happy. All the world suffer; and I, who deserve the severest discipline, feel joys so continual and so great that I can scarce contain them.

I would willingly ask of God a part of your sufferings, but that I know my weakness, which is so great that if He left me one moment to myself I should be the most wretched man alive. And yet I know not how He can leave me alone, because faith gives me as strong a conviction as sense can do that He never forsakes us until we have first forsaken Him. Let us fear to leave Him. Let us be always with Him. Let us live and die in His presence.

Brother Lawrence
d. 1691
(from *The Practice of the*
Presence of God)

CELEBRATING BEAUTY

Because of the light of the moon,
Silver is found on the moor;
Because of the light of the sun,
There is gold on the walls of the poor.

98

Because of the light of the stars,
Planets are found in the stream;
Because of the light in your eyes,
There is love in the depths of my dream.
Francis Carlin

When a sudden ray of sun or a moonbeam falls on a dreary street, it makes no difference what it illumines—a broken bottle on the ground, a fading flower in a field, or the flaxen blonde hair of a child's head. The object is transformed and the viewer is transfixed. Celebrate that moment of beauty and take it with you in your memory. It is God's gift to you.

There is an old saying: "Man is the measure of all things." This statement was never more applicable than in the realm of recognizing what is beautiful in life. We all measure what is beautiful by the effect things have upon us, according to how they seem to be with us. What seems beautiful to one person may not be to another, or even to the same person at a different time. There is another old saying: "Beauty is in the eye of the beholder." In other words, beauty is subjective or relative to individual judgment and taste. It is never "fixed." No one can question its validity because it is dependent upon the state we are in, not necessarily upon the object we are viewing.

Luci Swindoll

One of my favorite devotional writers was Englishman J. B. Phillips. He was one of the first to write a paraphrase of the New Testament, which, in my opinion, is still one of the best.

He also wrote books. One of my favorites is a little book entitled, simply, *Good News*. I blew dust off it just recently and found an interesting statement about being happy.

"Blessed" in the authorized version is very nearly the equivalent of our modern word "happy." So that Jesus, in effect, gives us a recipe for happiness in the Beatitudes. So as to make the revolutionary character of His recipe more apparent, I will quote first a little version of my own, of what most non-Christian people think.

They think: "Happy are the pushers, for they get on in the world. Happy are the hard-boiled, for they never let life hurt them. Happy are they who complain, for they get their own way in the end. Happy are the blasé, for they never worry over their sins. Happy are the slave drivers, for they get results. Happy are the knowledgable men of the world, for they know their way around. Happy are the troublemakers, for they make people take notice of them."

But Jesus said, "How happy are the humble-minded, for the kingdom of heaven is theirs. How happy are those who know what sorrow means, for they will be given courage and comfort. Happy are those who claim nothing, for the whole earth will belong to them. Happy are those who are hungry and thirsty for goodness, for they will be satisfied. Happy are the merciful, for they will have mercy shown to them. Happy are the utterly sincere, for they will see God. Happy are those who make peace, for they will be known as sons of God.

To be totally honest about it, happiness is really not that complicated. I'm convinced with all my heart (and I find that it works for me) that if my relationship with the living Lord is in place by faith in Jesus Christ, if I take His perspective and look at my life as it unfolds in the valleys as well as on the mountains—it's amazing!—happiness accompanies me.

But when I roll up my sleeves and take on life (including God) with grim determination that says, "I'm going to get what I want," I find that I sometimes get it, but happiness is never a by-product. Never. In fact, those are some of the darkest days of my life. Happiness eludes me—just as it does everyone else. The only way we can enjoy life is to find God's gift of happiness in Jesus Christ.

Charles R. Swindoll

Jesus Christ said:

Happy are those who realize their spiritual poverty: they have already entered the kingdom of Reality.
Happy are they who bear their share of the world's pain: in

the long run they will know more happiness than those
who avoid it.

Happy are those who accept life and their own limitations:
they will find more in life than anybody.

Happy are those who long to be truly "good": they will fully
realize their ambition.

Happy are those who are ready to make allowances and to
forgive: they will know the love of God.

Happy are those who are real in their thoughts and feelings:
in the end they will see the ultimate Reality, God.

Happy are those who help others to live together: they will
be known to be doing God's work.

It is quite plain that Christ is setting up ideals of different
quality from those commonly accepted. He is outlining the
sort of human characteristics which may fairly be said to be
co-operating with the purpose of Life, and He is by implication exposing the conventional mode of living which is at
heart based on self-love and leads to all kinds of unhappiness.

It should be noticed that this "recipe" for happy and constructive living is of universal application. It cuts across differ-
ences of temperament and variations in capacity. It outlines
the kind of character which is possible for *any* man, gifted or
relatively ungifted, strong or weak, clever or slow in the up-
take. Once more we find Christ placing His finger not upon
the externals, but upon the vital internal attitude.

It should also be noted that although we have called His
definitions "revolutionary" they are not fantastic. Indeed a
great many people probably realize that in following them
men would become their real selves and not the greedy, com-
petitive, self-loving characters that cause so many of the
world's troubles. Christ is restoring the true order, which man
can recognize as true, He is not imposing a set of arbitrary
regulations.

J. B. Phillips

As the hart panteth after the water brooks,
so panteth my soul after thee, O God.

My soul thirsteth for God, for the living God:
   when shall I come and appear before God?
My tears have been my meat day and night,
   while they continually say unto me,
     Where is thy God?
When I remember these things,
   I pour out my soul in me:
     for I had gone with the multitude,
       I went with them to the house of God,
   with the voice of joy and praise,
     with a multitude that kept holyday.
Why art thou cast down, O my soul,
   and why art thou disquieted in me?
     hope thou in God. . . .
Deep calleth unto deep at the noise of thy waterspouts:
   all thy waves and thy billows are gone over me.
Yet the Lord will command his loving-kindness
   in the daytime,
     and in the night his song shall be with me,
     and my prayer unto the God of my life.

Psalm 42:1–8

If anyone would tell you the shortest, surest way to happiness and all perfection, he must tell you to make it a rule to yourself to thank and praise God for everything that happens to you. For it is certain that whatever seeming calamity happens to you, if you thank and praise God for it, you turn it into a blessing.

William Law
1686–1761

Joy sometimes needs pain to give it birth. Fanny Crosby could never have written her beautiful hymn, "I shall see Him face to face," were it not for the fact that she had never looked upon the green fields nor the evening sunset nor the kindly twinkle in her mother's eye. It was the loss of her own vision that helped her to gain her remarkable spiritual discernment.

It is the tree that suffers that is capable of polish. When the woodman wants some curved lines of beauty in the grain he cuts down some maple that has been gashed by the axe and twisted by the storm. In this way he secures the knots and the hardness that take the gloss.

It is comforting to know that sorrow tarries only for the night; it takes its leave in the morning. A thunderstorm is very brief when put alongside the long summer day. "Weeping may endure for the night but joy cometh in the morning."

Songs in the Night

> There is a peace that cometh after sorrow,
> Of hope surrendered, not of hope fulfilled;
> A peace that looketh not upon tomorrow,
> But calmly on a tempest that it stilled.
> A peace that lives not now in joy's excesses,
> Nor in the happy life of love secure;
> But in the unerring strength the heart possesses,
> Of conflicts won while learning to endure,
> A peace there is, in sacrifice secluded,
> A life subdued, from will and passion free;
> 'Tis not the peace that over Eden brooded,
> But that which triumphed in Gethsemane.

Compiled by Mrs. Charles E. Cowman

HIS JOY IN YOU

Prayer is intimate communion Person to person. When we abide in God, listening receptively, we experience the ecstasy of joy. Let the word stand—*ecstasy.* It is the intense emotion which bursts within us when the Lord breaks through. Then we can say with Pascal, "Joy! Joy! Unspeakable joy!"

It was this spiritual ecstasy that Peter affirmed in the early church: "Without having seen him you love him; though you do not now see him [with eye perception] you believe in him [heart and mind perception through prayer] and rejoice with unutterable and exalted joy" (1 Pet. 1:8).

In a much deeper way, we can express about Christ what Montaigne said of a friend: "How is it that we were so much to one another, you and I? It was because you were you and I was I." Grim people like us need the joy only a Savior can give. And only the great "I am" can meet our needs. We can echo Charles Kingsley's simple assurance when asked how he took the pressure in his life. "I had a friend" was his only reply. Jesus, the vine, draws the joy from the reservoir of the Eternal and sends it into our thirsty branches.

My friend's parting benedictory encouragement is now my deepest prayer for you. I pray it in the context of Jesus' triumphant "I am" promise: "I am the vine, you are the branches." "Abide in me, and I in you . . . that my joy may be in you, and that your joy may be full."

Whatever you do, don't miss the joy!

Lloyd J. Ogilvie

Joyful, joyful, we adore Thee,
God of glory, Lord of love;
Hearts unfold like flowers before Thee,
Opening to the sun above.
Melt the clouds of sin and sadness,
Drive the dark of doubt away;
Giver of immortal gladness,
Fill us with the light of day.

Henry Van Dyke

I could see the smoke curling out of our chimney as I opened the grape-stake gate that had kept the sheep from wandering in decades past. I looked forward to putting on some dry jeans and getting as close as possible to that fire.

It was time to put *Gift from the Sea* and the five little shells back on the bookshelf until our next encounter. I wondered what the macho men who read *The Double Win* would think about an ex-navy carrier-based pilot who quotes Anne Morrow Lindbergh? *Well, never mind,* I shrugged. *I enjoy quiche, too!*

The children were helping Susan set the redwood picnic table on the enclosed porch as I walked in, padding across the tile floor in my wet socks.

"We thought you got lost," Susan teased. "The boys were about ready to organize a search party."

"It was such a beautiful sunset, I decided to spend a couple of hours just relaxing and meditating," I responded.

"You really need to stop and smell the roses more," she said. "You've been hitting it hard lately."

I went in and sat by the fire. I hoped I could honestly believe that I was learning that "hitting it hard" and "chasing it" were philosophies to be discarded like a caterpillar sheds its cocoon to become a monarch butterfly. Butterflies, I remembered, don't "hit it hard"; they float with a light touch.

As I studied the faces of my beautiful wife and our six children, I realized it was Father's Day. I marveled at the individuality and uniqueness in each of our children. Like monarch butterflies, all but two of them were flying free on their own. What a joy for all of us to be together again, if only for the weekend.

We sat down to our meal and as I finished saying grace, I added a silent thank-you of my own to God for teaching me that the greatest gift a father can receive is in giving his love to his family.

Before the fire burned low, I promised myself, I would let each of them know how rich I was from sharing in their lives. And I would pen these thoughts:

Sharing . . . caring . . . giving . . . receiving. Getting the most of life as we give our best to others.

The Double Win!

Denis Waitley

May the grace of Christ our Saviour,
　and the Father's boundless love,
With the Holy Spirit's favor,
　rest upon us from above.

Thus may we abide in union
    with each other and the Lord,
And possess in sweet communion
    joys which earth cannot afford.

John Newton
1725–1807

JOY

Joy has much more to do with the affections than with reason. To the man with a family, his wife and children call out and sustain his delights much more than his intellect could ever stimulate. Standing before a cradle a father seems face to face with the attributes of the everlasting Being who has infused His tenderness and love into the babe. The power of rejoicing is always a fair test of a man's moral condition. No man can be happy on the outside who is already unhappy on the inside. If a sense of guilt weighs down the soul, no amount of pleasure on the outside can compensate for the loss of joy on the inside. As sorrow is attendant on sin, so joy is the companion of holiness.

Joy can be felt in both prosperity and adversity. In prosperity it consists not in the goods we enjoy but in those we hope for; not in the pleasures we experience but in the promise of those we believe without our seeing. Riches may abound, but those for which we hope are the kind that moths do not eat, rust consume, nor thieves break through and steal. Even in adversity there can be joy in the assurance that the Divine Master Himself died through the Cross as the condition of His Resurrection.

If joy be uncommon today it is because there are timid souls who have not the courage to forget themselves and to make sacrifices for their neighbor, or else because the narrower sympathies make the brighter things of the world to come appear as vanities. As the pull from the belief in God and the salvation of the soul fades from life, so also joy vanishes and one returns to the despair of the heathens. The old Greeks and Romans always saw a shadow across their path and a skeleton at their feet. It was no surprise that one day a Roman who had nothing to live for, nothing to hope for, entered his bath and opened a vein and so bled quietly and painlessly to death. A famous Greek poet once said of life that it was better not to be born, and the next best thing was to quit life as soon as possible. All this is at the other extreme from St. Paul, who said: "Rejoice in the Lord always and again I say, rejoice."

Bishop Fulton J. Sheen

In a sermon, I said, "Jesus was the most joyful person who ever lived." Afterward a friend took me to task, saying "Jesus was not joyful, He was a 'man of sorrows and acquainted with grief' (*see* Isaiah 53:3)." But we must know that joy and sorrow are not contradictory words. Jesus did experience sorrow—and disappointment—and pain—and frustration—and loneliness. But listen to His own words: "These things have I spoken unto you, that my joy might remain in you, and that your joy might be full" (John 15:11).

Just as all the water in the world cannot quench the fire of the Holy Spirit, neither can all the troubles and tragedies of the world overwhelm the joy which the Spirit brings into the human heart. There is a Cross at the heart of the Christian faith, but that does not alter the fact that there is joy in the heart of the Christian. On the day of Pentecost, observers thought that the Christians were drunk. Instead they were filled with such joy they could not contain themselves.

Sometimes we confuse joy and pleasure. Pleasure depends on circumstances and pleasures can come and go. What brings pleasure today may not bring it tomorrow. But joy is an experience that does not come and go. It is deep and real. Jesus said to His disciples, ". . . In the world ye shall have tribulation; but be of good cheer: I have overcome the world" (John 16:33). In spite of what happens, the Christian has optimistic faith in God's triumph. The Christian even looks at death and sees eternal joy beyond.

The basic enemies of joy are worry, guilt, and the fear of defeat. When one rejoices in the Lord, worries are overcome, forgiveness is a real experience, and one possesses the assurance that God's cause will triumph.

Charles L. Allen

Joy is distinctly a Christian word and a Christian thing. It is the reverse of happiness. Happiness is the result of what happens of an agreeable sort. Joy has its springs deep down inside. And that spring never runs dry, no matter what happens. Only Jesus gives that joy. He had joy, singing its music within, even under the shadow of the cross. It is an unknown word and thing except as He has sway within.

S. D. Gordon

YOU CAN NEVER HAVE TOO MUCH JOY

Sometimes we are almost afraid to enjoy the peace of Christ because we are sure something will come crashing in and scatter that peace like a shattered pane of glass. People sometimes say that things are going so well they are sure something is going to happen.

Luis Palau talked about this attitude in his book *The Moment to Shout.* He was driving to the office and he heard a preacher on the radio discussing the fruits of the spirit—love, joy, peace, patience, kindness, goodness, faithfulness, gentleness, self-control. The Bible says, "Against such there is no law." Palau was waiting at the red light and the preacher said, "You know what that means. . . . It means there is no law against loving too much!"

Palau said he almost missed the green light.

The preacher added, "God will never come alongside you and say, 'You have loved enough. You'd better put the brakes on awhile.' There is no law against love!" Then he added, "You can never be too joyful in Jesus Christ. God is never going to say, 'You have had too much fun for a while, so now I'm going to cool it for you.'"

Jesus said, "Rejoice always." Too much of the time Christians are sour-apple people. We think being happy is superficial. But God says there is no law against joy. We can have as much of it as we want, if we allow the indwelling Christ to control us.

We can have it all . . . all the time. But we have to avoid thoughts like, "It has been peaceful for the last three weeks. Now it's time to worry a bit!"

God says, "Rejoice always, and again I say, rejoice!"

Mary C. Crowley

O Thou Supreme! most secret and most present, most beautiful and strong! What shall I say, my God, my Life, my Holy Joy? What shall any man say when he speaks of thee?

Saint Augustine
A.D. 354–430

The happiness which brings enduring worth to life is not the superficial happiness that is dependent on circumstances. It is the happiness and contentment that fills the soul even in the midst of the most distressing of circumstances and the most bitter environment. It is the kind of happiness that grins when things go wrong and smiles through the tears. The happiness for which our souls ache is one undisturbed by success or failure, one which will root deeply inside us and give inward relaxation, peace and contentment, no matter what the surface problems may be. That kind of happiness stands in need of no outward stimulus.

Billy Graham

This is a cheerful world as I see it from my garden under the shadows of my vines. But if I were to ascend some high mountain and look out over the wide lands, you know very well what I would see: brigands on the highways, pirates on the sea, armies fighting, cities burning; in the amphitheaters men murdered to please applauding crowds; selfishness and cruelty and misery and despair under all roofs. It is a bad world, Donatus, an incredibly bad world. But I have discovered in the midst of it a quiet and holy people who have learned a great secret. They have found a joy which is a thousand times better than any pleasure of our sinful life. They are despised and persecuted, but they care not. They are masters of their souls. They have overcome the world. These people, Donatus, are the Christians—and I am one of them.

Saint Cyprian
(third-century martyr)

HE HATH GIVEN ME REST BY HIS SORROW, AND LIFE BY HIS DEATH

Now I saw in my dream, that the highway up which Christian was to go was fenced on either side by a wall, and the wall was called Salvation. Up this way, therefore, did burdened Christian run, but not without great difficulty, because of the load on his back.

He ran thus till he came to a place somewhat ascending; and upon that place stood a Cross, and a little below, in the bottom, a sepulchre. So I saw in my dream that just as Christian came up with the Cross, his burden loosed from off his shoulders, and fell off his back, and began to tumble, and so continued to do till it came to the mouth of the sepulchre, where it fell in, and I saw it no more.

Then was Christian glad and lightsome, and said with a merry heart, 'He hath given me rest by His sorrow, and life by

His death.' Then he stood still a while to look and wonder; for it was very surprising to him that the sight of the Cross should thus ease him of his burden. He looked therefore, and looked again, even till the springs that were in his head sent the waters down his cheeks. Now as he stood looking and weeping, behold, three shining ones came to him, and saluted him with 'Peace be to thee.' So the first said to him, 'Thy sins be forgiven thee'; the second stripped him of his rags, and clothed him with a change of raiment; the third also set a mark on his forehead; and gave him a roll with a seal upon it, which he bid him look on as he ran, and that he should give it in at the celestial gate; so they went their way. Then Christian gave three leaps for joy, and went on singing.

John Bunyan
1628–1688
(from *The Pilgrim's Progress*)

There is nothing—no circumstance, no trouble, no testing—that can ever touch me until, first of all, it has gone past God and past Christ, right through to me. If it has come that far, it has come with a great purpose, which I may not understand at the moment. But as I refuse to become panicky, as I lift up my eyes to him and accept it as coming from the throne of God for some great purpose of blessing to my own heart, no sorrow will ever disturb me, no trial will ever disarm me, no circumstance will cause me to fret, for I shall rest in the joy of what my Lord is. That is the rest of victory.

Alan Redpath

REMEMBERING CORRIE TEN BOOM'S FAMILY

When I arrived in Haarlem, Corrie's hometown, it was a cold, freezing, rainy day, but the colorful architecture and the personality of this thriving market town captured my imagination. As I walked up her street, the Barteljorisstraat, my mind went back into the past. Standing by the bakery oppo-site the narrow, quaint, Dutch house that had belonged to the ten Booms, I could visualize Papa ten Boom coming to the door of his watch shop to greet his customers. I imagined Betsie arriving on her bicycle, ladened with groceries—Corrie opening the side door to help her, and their laughing together, enjoying the moment.

My mind then flashed to a different scene—down the cob-blestone streets came the thunder of German tanks and goose-stepping Nazi soldiers. From that same little peaceful house I could see the ten Booms led away to prison by the Gestapo. . . .

Returning to the present scene around me, I saw children laughing and playing in the rain, shoppers gossiping, and the very same brightly painted street organ (drawn by a gaily bedecked horse) that Corrie would have known as a child, playing a haunting Schubert melody.

I thought, *Do these people have any idea of what actually took place in the house across the street; the Jews that were saved; the suffering of the ten Booms; their undaunted faith in Christ?*

Perhaps some of the older people might remember, but the price of freedom—which is so often taken for granted—is one that is paid so that future generations can live in peace.

Like Corrie, if we really take Him at His word and believe that He is with us always, then nothing that is evil in this life can conquer us.

There are many lessons to be learned from the courageous ten Booms, among them, the value of a consecrated Christian home and the joy—the absolute joy—of serving our Lord with the strength that *He* gives through His Word.

Joan Winmill Brown

O sing to the Lord a new song,
  for he has done marvelous things!
His right hand and his holy arm
  have gotten him victory.
The Lord has made known his victory,
  he has revealed his vindication in the sight of the nations.

He has remembered his steadfast love and faithfulness
   to the house of Israel
All the ends of the earth have seen
   the victory of our God

Psalm 98:1–3 RSV

It is a wonderful thing to be really one with a risen and exalted Saviour, to be a member of Christ! Think what it involves. Can Christ be rich and I poor? Can your right hand be rich and your left poor? or your head be well fed while your body starves? Again, think of its bearing on prayer. Could a bank clerk say to a customer, "It was only your hand, not you that wrote that check"; or "I cannot pay this sum to your hand, but only to yourself"? No more can your prayers or mine be discredited if offered in the name of Jesus (i.e., not for the sake of Jesus merely, but on the ground that we are His, His members) so long as we keep within the limits of Christ's credit—a tolerably wide limit! If we ask for anything unscriptural, or not in accordance with the will of God, Christ Himself could not do that. But "if we ask any thing according to his will . . . we know that we have the petitions that we desired of him."

Hudson Taylor
1832–1905

THE PEACE OF GOD

Be careful for nothing; but in everything by prayer and supplication with thanksgiving let your requests be made known unto God. And the peace of God, which passeth all understanding, shall keep your hearts and minds through Christ Jesus. (Philippians 4:6, 7).

This is undoubtedly one of the noblest, greatest and most comforting statements which is to be found anywhere in any

113

extant literature. One is tempted to say that about many passages in the Scriptures, and yet from the standpoint of our personal lives in this world, and from the standpoint of practical experience, there is nothing that has greater comfort for God's people than these two verses. In them the apostle is continuing what is not only the major theme of this fourth chapter, but the major theme of the entire Epistle. He is concerned about the happiness and the joy of the members of the church at Philippi. He has written the specific exhortation that they should 'rejoice in the Lord always,' and again he says, 'rejoice.' In his great desire that these people might maintain that constant rejoicing in the Lord, the apostle has been considering various forces and factors that tend from time to time to rob the Christian of that joy and to bring him down to a lower level of Christian living. He has said: 'Let your long suffering—your forbearance—be known unto all men for the Lord is at hand.' He has shown how an unquiet spirit, a grasping desire to have our own way so frequently robs us of our joy.

D. Martyn Lloyd-Jones

To pursue joy is to lose it. The only way to get it is to follow steadily the path of duty, without thinking of joy, and then, like sheep, it comes most surely, unsought, and we 'being in the way' the angel of God, fair-haired joy, is sure to meet us.

Alexander Maclaren

In a message given at a Conference on Evangelism, in Lausanne, Switzerland, the respected English writer Malcolm Muggeridge told of his dramatic confrontation with Jesus Christ:

This is how I came to see my situation, in a sort of dream or vision; something more vivid and actual than most happenings and experiences. I am confined in the tiny dark dungeon of my ego; manacled with the appetites of the flesh, shackled with the inordinate demands of the will—a prisoner serving a life sentence with no hope of deliverance. Then I notice that high above me there is a window through which a faint glow of light comes filtering in. Seemingly so far way, so remote and inaccessible; yet I realize a window looking out onto eternity. Inside darkness, a place of fantasies and furies; outside, the white radiance of God's love shining through the universe, what the Apostle Paul called the glorious liberty of the children of God.

And the window? I know what that is too—the Incarnation. Time and eternity intersecting in a cross; now becoming Always. God revealing Himself as a man, and reaching down to us, in order that we, reaching up, may relate ourselves to Him. Now I observe that the window is not, after all, far away, but near at hand, and that seen through it everything makes sense; as it were, comes into sync, so that like the blind man whose sight Jesus restores, I can say: "One thing I know, that whereas I was blind, now I see. Thenceforth, whenever I am looking through the window I see life as being full of joy and hope and brotherliness. . . ."

Malcolm Muggeridge

Ye that do your Master's will,
Meek in heart be meeker still:
Day by day your sins confess,
Ye that walk in righteousness:
Gracious souls in grace abound,
Seek the Lord, whom ye have found.

He that comforts all that mourn
Shall to joy your sorrow turn:
Joy to know your sins forgiven,
Joy to keep the way to heaven,
Joy to win his welcome grace,
Joy to see Him face to face.

Charles Wesley
1707–1788

115

THE CHRISTIAN AND ANXIETY

Have you ever seen an anxious person who also exuded a spirit of joy? Yet both Paul and Jesus admonished the early Christians to be joyful. I don't read that either teacher taught that Christians are to evidence a fearful or anxious spirit. One of the shades of meaning in the word "blessed" which prefaces each of the Beatitudes in this very concept: "Be joyful" (see the Amplified Bible).

Over and over again the New Testament tells us that the hallmark of the Christian life is to be a joyous spirit. How can we be joyful if our souls are riddled with anxiety and worry? This is the idea Jesus was seeking to convey here. Along with freeing us from the penalty of our sin at Calvary, Jesus also gave us the key to the marvelous freedom of the joyful spirit. This joy or happiness does not come to us because we make it the object of our pursuit. Rather, it is the by-product of the Christian life. As C. S. Lewis so aptly put it, we are "surprised by joy" when we yield control of our lives to the Master. Joy doesn't come from desperate seeking—it comes as a result of self-surrender.

D. Stuart Briscoe

FOR A CONTENTED LIFE

Health enough to make work a pleasure.
Wealth enough to support your needs.
Strength to battle with difficulties and overcome them.
Grace enough to confess your sins and forsake them.
Patience enough to toil until some good is accomplished.
Charity enough to see some good in your neighbour.

Love enough to move you to be useful and helpful to others.
Faith enough to make real the things of God.
Hope enough to remove all anxious fears concerning the
    future.

Johann Wolfgang von Goethe
1749–1832

ONLY THE WISE MAN

Only the wise man draws from life, and from every stage of it, its true savour, because only he feels the beauty, the dignity, and the value of life. The flowers of youth may fade, but the summer, the autumn, and even the winter of human existence, have their majestic grandeur, which the wise man recognizes and glorifies. To see all things in God; to make of one's own life a journey towards the ideal; to live with gratitude, with devoutness, with gentleness and courage;—this was the splendid aim of Marcus Aurelius. And if you add to it the humility which kneels, and the charity which gives, you have the whole wisdom of the children of God, the immortal joy which is the heritage of the true Christian.

Henri Frederic Amiel
1821–1881

THE WALK TO EMMAUS

It happened, on a solemn eventide,
Soon after he that was our surety died,
Two bosom friends, each pensively inclined,
The scene of all those sorrows left behind,
Sought their own village, busied, as they went,
In musings worthy of the great event:

117

They spake of him they loved, of him whose life,
Though blameless, had incurred perpetual strife,
Whose deeds had left, in spite of hostile arts,
A deep memorial graven on their hearts.
The recollection, like a vein of ore,
The farther traced, enriched them still the more;
They thought him, and they justly thought him, one
Sent to do more than He appeared t'have done;
To exalt a people, and to place them high
Above all else, and wondered he should die.
Ere yet they brought their journey to an end,
A Stranger joined them, courteous as a friend,
And asked them, with a kind engaging air,
What their affliction was, and begged a share.
Informed, he gathered up the broken thread,
And, truth and wisdom gracing all he said,
Explained, illustrated, and searched so well
The tender theme, on which they chose to dwell,
That reaching home, "The night," they said, "is near,
We must not now be parted, sojourn here."
The new acquaintance soon became a guest,
And, made so welcome at their simple feast,
He blessed the bread, but vanished at the word,
And left them both exclaiming, "'Twas the Lord!
Did not our hearts feel all he deigned to say,
Did they not burn within us by the way?"

William Cowper
1731–1800

There is but one way to tranquility and happiness. Let this
therefore be always ready at hand with thee, both when thou
wakest early in the morning, and when thou goest late to
sleep, to account no eternal thing thine own, but commit all
these to God.

Epictetus
A.D. 50–138

THOU ART WORTHY

It is a triumph song, sung in heaven. Listen! Can we catch its meaning?

"Worthy is the Lamb that hath been slain to receive the power, and riches, and wisdom, and might, and honour, and glory and blessing."

It is a song of joy and praise, the Hallelujah Chorus of the universe.

And who are the singers, there? Those redeemed out of "every tribe and tongue and people and nation," many of whom came from the furnace of affliction, but whose tears are for ever wiped away. It is the sublimation of all earth's "songs in the night," from hearts that suffer for and with their Lord.

The Christian sings, and sings in tribulation. Prison walls heard the praises of Paul and Silas, and Peter's epistles of suffering are the pages that tell of "joy unspeakable and full of glory."

The Christian is the greatest of all paradoxes: a being "corrupt and yet purified, mortal and yet immortal, fallen but yet exalted far above principalities and powers, sorrowful yet always rejoicing."

Charles Spurgeon

Lord, what a change within us one short hour
Spent in Thy presence will prevail to make!
What heavy burdens from our bosoms take,
What parched grounds refresh as with a shower!
We kneel, and all around us seems to lower;
We rise, and all, the distant and the near,
Stands forth in sunny outline brave and clear;
We kneel, how weak! we rise, how full of power!

119

Why, therefore, should we do ourselves this wrong
Or others, that we are not always strong,
That we are ever overborne with care,
That we should ever weak or heartless be,
Anxious or troubled, when with us is prayer,
And joy and strength and courage are with Thee!

Richard Chenevix Trench
1807–1886

Part Four

Encircled by His Caring

6

We are surrounded by His everlasting love, which is unlimited —unchanging.

If I take the wings of the morning,
  and dwell in the uttermost parts of the sea;
Even there shall thy hand lead me,
  and thy right hand shall hold me.

Psalm 139:9–10

DAY BY DAY

Since we cannot get tomorrow's strength until tomorrow, how futile it is to try today to carry tomorrow's burden! With the burden will come the strength and the guidance. Wasn't this what Jesus meant when He said, "Don't fret about tomorrow. Today's cares are quite enough for today"? And let us not forget that He also said, "I am with you all the days, even unto the end."

By all means let us *plan* ahead, but let us *live* a day at a time, thinking positively, looking with faith and trust at God and committing ourselves wholly to Him Who loves, understands, forgives, accepts and empowers.

> Every day is a fresh beginning;
>   Listen, my soul, to the glad refrain,
> And, spite of old sorrow and older sinning,
>   And puzzles forecasted, and possible pain,
>   Take heart with the day and begin again.

After all, did not Jesus teach us to pray, "Give us *this* day our daily bread"? And day by day He will give us all the other things that we need. No one knows better than He that man does not live by bread alone.

Leslie D. Weatherhead

LIVING A DAY AT A TIME

I compare the troubles which we have to undergo in the course of the year to a great bundle of sticks, far too large for us to lift. But God does not require us to carry the whole at once. He mercifully unties the bundle, and gives us first one stick, which we are to carry today, and then another, which we are to carry tomorrow, and so on. This we might easily manage, if we would only take the burden appointed for us each day; but we choose to increase our troubles by carrying yesterday's stick over again today, and adding tomorrow's burden to our load, before we are required to bear it.

John Newton
1725–1807

Perhaps the greatest lesson which the lives of literary men teach us, is told in a single word—WAIT! Every man must patiently bide his time. He must wait.

We seem to live in the midst of a battle—there is such a din, such a hurrying to and fro. In the streets of a crowded city it is difficult to walk slowly. You feel the rushing of the crowd and rush with it onward. In the press of our life it is difficult to be calm. In this stress of wind and tide, all professions seem to drag their anchors, and are swept out into the main. The voices of the present say—Come! But the voices of the past say—Wait! With calm and solemn footsteps the rising tide bears against the rushing torrent up stream, and pushes back the hurrying waters. With no less calm and solemn footsteps, nor less certainty, does a great mind bear up against public opinion, and push back its hurrying stream. Therefore, should every man wait—should bide his time. Not in listless idleness, not in useless pastime, not in querulous dejection, but in constant, steady endeavours, always willing and fulfilling, and accomplishing his task, that when the occasion comes he may be equal to the occasion. And if it never comes, what matters it to the world whether I or you, or another man, did such a deed, or wrote such a book, so be it the deed and book were well done.

Henry Wadsworth Longfellow
1819–1892

Be not anxious about little things, if thou wouldst learn to trust God with thine all. Act upon faith in little things;

125

commit thy daily cares and anxieties to Him, and He will strengthen thy faith for greater trials that may come. Rather, give thy whole self into God's Hands, and so trust Him to take care of thee in all lesser things, as being His, for His own sake, Whose thou art.

Edward B. Pusey

HURRY, IMPATIENCE, AND TRUST

I am beginning to get a sneaking suspicion that some things will only come to us by waiting—that some things will never happen for us because we are in too big a hurry to let the time go by in which they can come true. We are not very patient people.

I often talk with people who firmly believe that God has some rich and deep purpose for their lives. It is evident they are sincere in their willingness and desire to find and fulfill that plan. But they experience difficulty because they cannot seem to trust the God who has ordained such purposes to also bring it about in his good and providential timing. They can't believe that when that something finally does occur, it will be with such obvious rightness that they will almost blush to ever have doubted it would be. They will wonder why it was so difficult to continue the present path with dedication and joy until some new word came to them.

To be able to do so we must become aware that there is some other way of accounting for time. We must begin to hear, however faintly at first, the rhythm and movement of the One who set it all in motion when the world began.

Bob Benson

All God's great people have been ordinary people who counted on God's being with them in power.

Ray Ortlund

126

A mother once took her little boy to hear Paderewski, the great pianist. At the beginning there was simply a bare stage with a spotlight focused on the grand piano and bench. The mother and son had come half an hour early, and eventually the little boy got restless. Somehow, the mother got absorbed in reading the program, and when she finally looked up, his seat was empty! She looked everywhere around her, and he was nowhere to be seen.

Then—her heart was in her throat—suddenly she heard the sound of "Chopsticks." There he was on stage, in the spotlight, picking away on the long concert grand!

"Get him out of there!" came voices from the crowd.

"No!" cried a European accent from the wings, and the great Paderewski strode on stage. "Boy, keep going. I'll help you."

And he sat down on the bench next to the little fellow and began adding fabulous improvisations—chords, patterns, runs, and additional melodies—as the two of them entranced the packed house with "Variations on Chopsticks"!

> In the same way, the Spirit helps us in our weakness. We do not know what we ought to pray, but the Spirit himself intercedes for us with groans that words cannot express. And he who searches our hearts knows the mind of the Spirit, because the Spirit intercedes for the saints in accordance with God's will (Rom. 8:26,27).

When we pick out our pathetic little prayers, suddenly we are not alone. Someone has come alongside us, and we have moved into a duet of greatness beyond our dreams.

Anne Ortlund

Father, in Thy mysterious presence kneeling,
    Fain would our souls feel all Thy kindling love;
For we are weak, and need some deep revealing
    Of trust and strength and calmness from above.

Lord, we have wandered forth through doubt and sorrow,
  And Thou hast made each step an onward one;
And we will ever trust each unknown morrow,—
  Thou wilt sustain us till its work is done.

In the heart's depths a peace serene and holy
  Abides; and when pain seems to have its will,
Or we despair, O may that peace rise slowly,
  Stronger than agony, and we be still!

Now, Father, now, in Thy dear presence kneeling,
  Our spirits yearn to feel Thy kindling love:
Now make us strong, we need Thy deep revealing
  Of trust and strength and calmness from above.

Samuel Johnson
1696–1772

We look into outer space, and because we cannot "see" a God we can touch, a God we can comprehend with our rational intellects, we invent new gods to take his place, all the little gods of technocracy, little gods who have eyes and see not, ears and hear not, hands and touch not, and who have nothing to say to us in the times of our deepest need.

Montaigne saw this and wrote, "O senseless man who cannot make a worm, and yet makes gods by dozens." We have been doing this for centuries and perhaps only the coming of the Kingdom will stop this futile activity.

Non-linear space/time is more easily understood by poets and saints than by reasonable folk. Back somewhere around the end of the eleventh century, Hildevert of Lavardin wrote:

> God is over all things,
> under all things,
> outside all,
> within, but not enclosed,
> without, but not excluded,
> above, but not raised up,
> below, but not depressed,

> wholly above, presiding,
> wholly without, embracing,
> wholly within, filling.

And that says all that needs saying.

Madeleine L'Engle

I, DANIEL

Over and over again, the psalm I had learned at my father's knee came into my prayers: "Even though I walk through the valley of the shadow of death, I fear no evil; for Thou art with me."

As I was praying, there was a tap on the door of my cell, and a face appeared at the small, barred window. It was King Darius. His face was distraught, the furrows in his brow deep with anguish. I wanted to reach out and comfort him, but there was a strong barricade between us with no room for a hand to be extended.

He said, "Daniel, I am so sorry for all of this. May your God, whom you worship continually, deliver you. I am going to spend tonight in fasting for you."

With those words he disappeared. It was gratifying to think that this new ruler would even acknowledge that my Lord was able to save me.

At that point I had no assurance what the hours before the dawn would hold for me. There were no visions, no visits from angels, only the quiet peace that my life was in Jehovah's hands.

However, that is not to say that I did not pray for protection! I was very tired by the time the guards came to lead me to the den. The cell was not large enough for me to recline and the tension of the past hours had left me in a state of exhaustion.

The roar of the hungry lions became almost deafening as we approached the large square cavern which had been dug deep below the surface of the earth. It was open from above, wide enough for several victims to be thrown in at a time, deep enough that the lions could not climb out. Surrounding this hole was a wall about as high as my chest. One could stand there and look far down into the den.

We stood for a moment, my four stalwart guards and I, and peered into the caverns. Below, about ten beasts were pacing, shaking their mighty bodies restlessly, growling, and baring their sharp teeth at the humans staring at them from above. An overwhelming gamy odor rose to meet our nostrils.

I thought I had never seen such huge animals in my life. A blow from one powerful paw could down a fully armed man. Those jaws could snap off an arm like a twig on a tree.

The guards were anxious to finish their unpleasant duty and leave the scene. They stared down for a few moments, then picked me up and threw me over the side.

In a split second, I thought, "My old bones will break before the lions touch me."

However, at that very moment I felt the softness of gentle arms surrounding my body. I saw nothing except a light that blinded me with its brilliance.

When I opened my eyes again, I was resting upon the reclining body of a lion, its shaggy fur providing me with all the soft comfort of a royal pillow. The same animals who just moments before had been ready to devour me now lay about me like oversized house cats contented in front of a warm fire. One huge animal stood in front of me, cocking his head to one side and then another. Evidently satisfied with what he saw— one harmless old man—he rubbed the broad side of his enormous head against my leg, stirring the circulation in my body with the motion. The others looked at me for a while, and then retired to their corners to sprawl in contented slumber. I reached out and ran my fingers through their tangled manes; what had been growls a moment before were now loud purrs. They licked my arms and hands with their rough tongues and gently placed their massive paws in my lap. I've never seen friendlier creatures.

"Lord, Lord," I laughed, "thank you for the decree of Darius and for sending your angels to guard me." What a story I would have to tell Mishael! But how will anyone ever believe this?

And with that, I fell asleep.

The next morning I was awakened by a voice calling to me

from the opening above the den. It was Darius. He said, "O Daniel, servant of the living God, was your God able to deliver you from the lions?"

I stood up, rested after one of the best night's sleep I had enjoyed in a long time, and called back, "Your Majesty, live forever!" (It was, after all, my duty to answer him with the respect due his position.) "My God has sent his angel to shut the lions' mouths, for I am innocent before God, nor, sir, have I wronged you."

I could hear him laugh and clap his hands. In a few moments a basket was lowered. I said goodbye to my animal friends and was lifted out of the den.

The king embraced me with tears rolling down his cheeks. He kept saying, "You haven't a scratch upon you. Your God is a powerful God!"

Carole C. Carlson
(from *A Light in Babylon*)

God is our refuge and strength,
    a very present help in trouble.
Therefore will not we fear, though the earth be removed,
    and though the mountains be carried into the midst of the
        sea;
Though the waters thereof roar and be troubled,
    though the mountains shake with the swelling thereof.
        Selah.
There is a river, the streams whereof shall make glad the city
        of God,
    the holy place of the tabernacles of the Most High.
God is in the midst of her; she shall not be moved:
    God shall help her, and that right early.
The heathen raged, the kingdoms were moved:
    he uttered his voice, the earth melted.
The Lord of hosts is with us;
    the God of Jacob is our refuge. Selah.
Come, behold the works of the Lord,
    what desolations he hath made in the earth.

He maketh wars to cease unto the end of the earth;
    he breaketh the bow, and cutteth the spear in sunder;
    he burneth the chariot in the fire.
Be still, and know that I am God:
    I will be exalted among the heathen,
    I will be exalted in the earth.
The Lord of hosts is with us;
    the God of Jacob is our refuge.

Psalm 46

NEVER GIVE UP

The great Russian writer, Solzhenitsyn, tells the bravest story I've ever heard to encourage us not to give up. In the Russian prison where he was, no one was allowed to speak. There was nothing to read, and no encouragement of any kind to sustain life. He said the strain and repression from this atmosphere had set in so badly that he thought, *I will never get out of here.* So he considered taking his own life. He knew that if he tried to escape he would be shot, but he thought, *At least, that will be the end of that!*

His faith would not allow him to do that, though. When day came, he was taken out early in the morning to work and when a break in the work day came, he sat under a tree. He even placed his hand behind him, up against the tree he leaned against, ready to push off and run. Just then a shadow came across the grass and a fellow prisoner sat down beside him. They could speak no words, but he looked into the eyes of the new man who had recently come as a prisoner and saw something he had never seen in any face in prison before—a message of love and concern.

As their eyes locked in silence, they started communicating in their souls and the prisoner took a step forward and drew a cross on the ground with a stick.

Solzhenitsyn said new hope surged within him at that moment. Jesus does love me. He is in command. It is not hopeless!

Three days later he was released from that prison. At his release he learned that many people had been praying for him. He knew with powerful certainty that God is sovereign and there is still hope.

We mustn't give up! We might be the one to communicate hope to someone else, maybe by a gesture, maybe without words. We must love and pray and hold one another up.

Mary C. Crowley

How easy it is for me to live with you, Lord!
How easy it is for me to believe in you!
When my mind is distraught and my reason fails,
When the cleverest people do not see further than this
        evening what must be done tomorrow
You grant me the clear confidence
    that you exist, and that you will take care
    that not all the ways of goodness are stopped.
    At the height of earthly fame I gaze with wonder
    at that path through hopelessness—
    to this point from which even I have been able
    to convey to men some reflection of the Light
    which comes from you.
    And you will enable me to go on doing
    as much as needs to be done.
    And in so far as I do not manage it—
    that means that you have allotted the task to others.

Alexander Solzhenitsyn

We live at a time in history when the forces of evil are strong, when peace and civilisation and Christianity often seem endangered. On the other hand, religious faith is making progress in unexpected ways, while brave and resolute men and women throughout the world are striving for goodwill and trying to win a happier future for the human race. To dedicate to such ends whatever of influence we possess, to endure through the darkest days with serene courage, to think little of our own needs and much of our neighbor's, to be unashamed in our religion and frank in making the FATHER'S Will our supreme rule in conduct—to do that is to fulfil the teaching of Good Friday, to follow so far as we may the supreme example of the Crucified, and to share in the triumph of the Cross.

For after nineteen centuries the Cross remains the Sign of victory, and in this Sign we shall conquer.

From the leading article in The London Times
Good Friday, 1933

I will lift up mine eyes unto the hills,
　from whence cometh my help.
My help cometh from the Lord,
　which made heaven and earth.
He will not suffer thy foot to be moved:
　he that keepeth thee will not slumber.
Behold, he that keepeth Israel
　shall neither slumber nor sleep.
The Lord is thy keeper:
　the Lord is thy shade
　　upon thy right hand.
The sun shall not smite thee by day,
　nor the moon by night.
The Lord shall preserve thee from all evil:
　he shall preserve thy soul.
The Lord shall preserve thy going out
　and thy coming in
　　from this time forth, and even for evermore.

Psalm 121

THE FOOT-PATH TO PEACE

To be glad of life because it gives you the chance to love and to work and to play and to look up at the stars—to be satisfied with your possessions but not contented with yourself until you have made the best of them—to despise nothing in the world except falsehood and meanness, and to fear nothing except cowardice—to be governed by your admirations rather than by your disgusts; to covet nothing that is your neighbor's except his kindness of heart and gentleness of manners—to think seldom of your enemies, often of your friends, and every day of Christ; and to spend as much time as you can, with body and with spirit, in God's out-of-doors—these are little guide-posts on the foot-path to peace.

Henry Van Dyke

To be at peace. The longing for peace must have come to us with the dawn of reason, as soon as man was able to ask himself, 'What do I want?' He knew it first perhaps in the passing of a storm, when the terrifying thunder and darkness rolled away, the sun came out on a rain-washed world and the birds sang again. Then when a fight with man or beast was over and he was still alive, and could get back to husbandry or rock-painting, work that absorbed and quieted him, made no noise and shed no blood, or when he went home at night to his cave and saw in the firelight his son asleep in the mother's arms. Or, supremely, when in a still and soundless world he waited in trembling awe for the rising of the sun, not knowing with certainty if the god would come again, only hoping, until he heard the first joyous cry of a bird and saw the slow lightening on the eastern horizon. Then would come peace, flooding his soul as the glory of his God once more dawned upon him.

Elizabeth Goudge

GOD'S GIFT OF PEACE

The peace *of* God is first and foremost peace *with* God; it is the state of affairs in which God, instead of being *against* us, is *for* us. No account of God's peace which does not start here can do other than mislead. One of the miserable ironies of our time is that whereas liberal and 'radical' theologians believe themselves to be re-stating the gospel for today, they have for the most part rejected the categories of wrath, guilt, condemnation, and the enmity of God, and so have made it impossible for themselves ever to present the gospel at all, for they cannot now state the basic problem which the gospel of peace solves.

The peace of God, then, primarily and fundamentally, is a new relationship of forgiveness and acceptance—and the source from which it flows is propitiation. When Jesus came to His disciples in the upper room at evening on His resurrection day, He said, 'Peace be unto you'; 'and when He had so said, He showed unto them His hands and His side'(John 20:19f). Why did He do that? Not just to establish His identity, but to remind them of the propitiatory death on the cross whereby He had made peace with His Father for them. Having suffered in their place, as their substitute, to make peace for them, He now came in His risen power to bring that peace to them. 'Behold the Lamb of God, which taketh away the sin of the world.' It is here, in the recognition that, whereas we are by nature at odds with God, and God with us, Jesus has 'made peace through the blood of His cross' (Colossians 1:20), that true knowledge of the peace of God begins.

J. I. Packer

Go on your way in peace.
Be of good courage.
Hold fast that which is good.
Render no man evil for evil.
Strengthen the fainthearted.
Support the weak.
Help and cheer the sick.
Honor all men.
Love and serve the Lord.
May the blessings of God be upon you
    and remain with you forever.

Benediction from Gloucester Cathedral

Miobi had come to a village where the people were doing nothing else but moan and wail. The fires were not lit, the goats were not milked, because all the villagers were expecting to be eaten shortly by the Monster on the Top of the Mountain.

This monster had the head of a crocodile and the body of a hippopotamus and a tail like a very fat snake, and smoke came from his fiery breath.

But Miobi said, "I will go up the mountain and challenge the monster."

There he was, sure enough.

But as the boy climbed and came nearer, the monster looked definitely smaller.

"This is very curious indeed," he said. "The further I run away from the monster, the larger it seems, and the nearer I am to it, the smaller it seems."

When the boy reached the cave, he found no monster—but a quiet little thing as small as a frog, which purred; and he brought it home as a pet.

When the villagers saw him return, they wanted to make a hero of him for killing the monster, but he explained just what had happened and how he had brought the monster home as a pet.

What was its name?

The monster answered, "I have many names. Some call me famine, and some pestilence; but the most pitiable of humans give me their own names."

It yawned and added, "But most people call me What-Might-Happen."

Is Jesus a tower-light of protection against this kind of fear? Yes, because Jesus is Light and that Light can melt and dispel these submerged incapacitating fantasies.

Sometimes it helps to write down one's fears, then hold them up one by one to the light of Christ's clear understanding. Never is Jesus as the Light of the World more clear than in these murky areas of our semiconscious fears, most of them unreal and psychotic. The trouble with the imaginary fears is that they can, if allowed to go on and on unchallenged, really destroy. As we talk over each fear on the list with Christ, He will illuminate for us some steps to expose them for what they really are. . . .

Catherine Marshall

CHRIST SPEAKS TO US
WHEN WE ARE FRIGHTENED

Pluck up thy courage, faint heart; what though thou be fearful, sorry and weary, and standeth in great dread of most painful torments, be of good comfort; for I myself have vanquished the whole world, and yet felt I far more fear, sorrow, weariness, and much more inward anguish too, when I considered my most bitter, painful Passion to press so fast upon me. He that is strong-hearted may find a thousand glorious valiant martyrs whose ensample he may right joyously follow. But thou now, O timorous and weak, silly sheep, think it sufficient for thee only to walk after me, which am thy shepherd and governor, and so mistrust thyself and put thy trust in me. Take hold on the hem of my garment, therefore; from thence shalt thou perceive such strength and relief to proceed. . . .

Sir Thomas More
(from *Treatise on the Passion*)
1478–1535

If you lose heart about your work,
remember that none of it is lost,
that the good of every good deed remains and breeds
and works on forever,
and that all that fails and is lost
is the outside shell of the thing.

Charles Kingsley
1819–1875

SEEMING DEFEAT

The platform of defeat and failure—do not fret about it. Do not quickly assume it is the end of the matter—it is not. Wait for God to work, and believe our Lord when He says the gates of hell shall not prevail against His kingdom.

I have often been impressed by the dramatic picture so simply disclosed in II Timothy 4—the last recorded words of Paul.

He knew his life was drawing to a close. If he had used physical sight only, he would have had to say, "My lifework has been a colossal failure." He, the saintliest of men, was in chains; he was brought thus before Nero, the vilest of men. One student of Nero's life has said of him, "He was only mud and blood." Yet Nero was on the throne, and Paul the saint a prisoner before him.

"At my first answer no man stood with me, but all men forsook me," Paul wrote later. What a disappointment! There were supposed to be stalwart saints in Rome at that time. His dear friends had deserted him. But not all. *"Notwithstanding the Lord stood with me."* Yea, there is one Friend who never fails us.

"This thou knowest, that all they which are in Asia be turned away from me"(II Tim. 1:15). Why, Asia comprised some of Paul's most cherished fruit! Years of his life had been spent to establish those young churches. And now, in the last epistle he wrote before he died, he says they had repudiated him. Doubtless his old enemies, the Judaizers, had influenced them.

What a melancholy picture! What a way to end a life of such self-sacrifice! Himself in bonds, shortly to be condemned and executed. His friends had deserted him. His spiritual children had repudiated him. Paul, your life is a colossal failure!

"Oh, no," he says quietly, using the eyes of faith. "I have fought a good fight . . . henceforth there is laid up for me a crown of righteousness." There is no defeat in those words.

141

And now we, nineteen centuries later, may be judges as to which saw correctly—Paul's eyes of faith, or the fleshly eye of sight? The eye of faith saw correctly.

The platform of seeming defeat and failure will conform us to His image in humility. If we wait patiently we shall some day see His power working in undreamed-of-ways. And we shall *know Him; as with Paul, the Lord will stand by us and strengthen us.*

Isobel Kuhn

If a man is centred upon himself the smallest risk is too great for him, because both success and failure can destroy him. If he is centred upon God, then no risk is too great, because success is already guaranteed—the successful union of Creator and creature, beside which every thing else is meaningless.

Morris L. West
(from *The Shoes of the Fisherman*)

And, behold, I am with thee, and will keep thee in all places whither thou goest, and will bring thee again into this land; for I will not leave thee, until I have done that which I have spoken to thee of (Gen. 28:15).

"With You"; not merely looking down out of the sky at you struggling in your work, but by your very side, closer than the nearest colleague, holding you by the hand, whispering words of strange power for you to use, and words of still stranger power for your own heart only, calming, and strengthening, and gladdening it; so that if you are "men wondered at" by others, you are a great deal more wondered at by yourself. You are so "marvellously helped," that you "never would have thought it!" No, of course not; but, you see, His thoughts towards you in your work were much better than yours, and you can say:

And now I find Thy promise true,
  Of perfect peace and rest;
I cannot sigh—I can but sing
  While leaning on Thy breast,
And leaving everything to Thee
  Whose ways are always best.
                    Frances Ridley Havergal

From Christian's Daily Challenge

He that dwelleth in the secret place of the Most High
  shall abide under the shadow of the Almighty.
I will say of the Lord, He is my refuge and my fortress:
  my God; in him will I trust.
Surely he shall deliver thee from the snare of the fowler,
  and from the noisome pestilence.
He shall cover thee with his feathers,
  and under his wings shalt thou trust:
  his truth shall be thy shield and buckler.
Thou shalt not be afraid for the terror by night;
  nor for the arrow that flieth by day;
Nor for the pestilence that walketh in darkness;
  nor for the destruction that wasteth at noonday.
A thousand shall fall at thy side,
  and ten thousand at thy right hand;
  but it shall not come nigh thee.
Only with thine eyes shalt thou behold
  and see the reward of the wicked.
Because thou hast made the Lord, which is my refuge,
  even the Most High, thy habitation;
There shall no evil befall thee,
  neither shall any plague come nigh thy dwelling.
For he shall give his angels charge over thee,
  to keep thee in all thy ways.
They shall bear thee up in their hands,
  lest thou dash thy foot against a stone.

Thou shalt tread upon the lion and adder:
the young lion and the dragon shalt thou trample under
feet.
Because he hath set his love upon me,
therefore will I deliver him:
I will set him on high,
because he hath known my name.
He shall call upon me, and I will answer him:
I will be with him in trouble;
I will deliver him, and honor him.
With long life will I satisfy him,
and show him my salvation.

Psalm 91

BECAUSE THERE IS A GOD

Now he had learnt to see the great, the eternal, and the infinite in everything; and naturally therefore, in order to see it, to revel in its contemplation, he flung aside the telescope through which he had hitherto been gazing over men's heads, and looked joyfully at the ever-changing, ever-grand, unfathomable, and infinite life around him. And the closer he looked at it, the calmer and happier he was. The terrible question that had shattered all his intellectual edifices in old days, the question: What for? had no existence for him now. To that question, What for? he had now always ready in his soul the simple answer: Because there is a God, that God without whom not one hair of a man's head falls.

Count Leo Tolstoy
1828–1910

For I am persuaded, that neither death, nor life, nor angels, nor principalities, nor powers, nor things present, nor things to come, nor height, nor depth, nor any other creature, shall be

able to separate us from the love of God, which is in Christ
Jesus our Lord.

Romans 8:38–39

NOR THINGS TO COME

Too risky, fear says,
But faith says, *"Nor things to come."*
Four little words that restore our perspective, cool our fever-
ish self-centeredness, unclench our fists, straighten our backs,
get us going again.

Nor things to come.

Always it is the future that we worry about most. Things
present we somehow cope with, however distressing. Nine-
tenths of fear hides in the future tense. Fear lives not in the
known, but in the unknown. Not in what is already here but in
what hasn't yet arrived. But see: "Neither . . . things present,
nor things to come."

Faith is always for the unexplored place, the experience we
have not yet had. "A man who already has something doesn't
need to hope and trust that he will get it" (Rom. 8:24 LB). Or
not get it. Faith is the force that starts our blood circulating,
our juices flowing, our thoughts and feet and hands moving.
Abraham "went out, not knowing whither he went." What he
did know was with Whom he went. That was enough.

From Genesis to Revelation, the good word is, "Fear not."
Neither things present.

Nor things to come.

That doesn't turn a Christian into a twittering Pollyanna.
But it should make one an unwavering optimist. It's the believer's birthright.

Stan Mooneyham

7

*Our Lord's comforting presence
brings hope for all our tomorrows.*

I do not know what the future holds
   Of joy or pain,
   Of loss or gain,
Along life's untrod way;
   But I believe
   I can receive
God's promised guidance day by day;
   So I securely travel on.

And if, at times, the journey leads
   Through waters deep,
   Or mountains steep,
I know this unseen Friend,
   His love revealing,
   His presence healing,
Walks with me to the journey's end;
   So I securely travel on.

Author Unknown

147

He had a round clerical hat, dusty and green with age. He put it on, gripped his umbrella in his left hand and held out his right to me. I held it and it was dry and rough and hot. 'My dear,' he said, 'I will pray for you every day of my life until I die.'

Then he abruptly let go of my hand, turned his back on me and stumbled down the steps that led from the front door to the drive. At the bottom he turned round again and looking into his face I noticed that when he was neither eager nor alarmed his eyes had the most extraordinary quietness in them. 'My dear,' he said, 'Love, your God, is a trinity. There are three necessary prayers and they have three words each. They are these, "Lord have mercy. Thee I adore. Into Thy hands." Not difficult to remember. If in times of distress you hold to these you will do well.' Then he lifted his hat and turned round again. I stood at the door and watched him go. He had a queer wavering sort of walk. He did not look back.

Elizabeth Goudge
(from *The Bird in the Tree*)

The little ship in which the disciples were tossed in the middle of the sea was being driven to and fro by a "contrary wind." Can't you imagine the chill of wet skin and clothing as the wind whirled around the men, destroying any possibility of directing the ship, and threatening to overturn it? Then suddenly the men caught sight of a form coming towards them. Could something be going wrong with their eyes? No, it was a man, but it couldn't be; it must be a ghost! Perhaps their teeth chattered with something more than cold, as sudden terror was added to their natural fear, and their screams arose above the sound of the wind and sea. There was no other boat in sight; there was no place from which help could come.

"But straightway Jesus spake unto them, saying, Be of good cheer; it is I; be not afraid" (*see* Matthew 14:27). I love the "straightway" because it portrays the gentleness and tenderness of Jesus and of God the Father. Jesus said He came to make known the Father. Jesus cared about quieting the fears immediately. Did He change the force of the waves and stop the wild wind right away? No, we know He didn't at this time. What then was the meaning of *be of good cheer, be not afraid* in that context? It carries us back to Psalms 46:1–3: "God is our refuge and strength, a very present help in trouble. Therefore will not we fear, though the earth be removed, and though the mountains be carried into the midst of the sea; though the waters thereof roar and be troubled, though the mountains shake with the swelling thereof." The reality of the presence of God with us, His tender love for us, and His trustworthiness as our Guide is to dispel our natural fear, even in the midst of storm and earthquake—while the waters are still roaring and the wind is still buffeting our faces and whipping our clothing around us. God is our Refuge during the time no visible change has come in the circumstances. Our complete trust is to be in Him alone, not merely in what we suddenly see Him doing for us. We are given moments of opportunity to demonstrate a steady trust.

Edith Schaeffer

We shall steer safely through every storm,
    so long as our heart is right,
our intention fervent, our courage steadfast,
    and our trust fixed on God.

François de Sales

What of the folk back home
that day
the sudden storm swept Galilee?
Knowing the violence of those storms,
the smallness of the craft,
did they

149

abandon themselves to grief,
or say,
"The One who sails with them
is He
Who made the storm-filled universe,
the height,
the depth,
the everywhere;
the storm is fierce,
the craft is small,
but
He is there!"?

Ruth Bell Graham

There are songs which can only be learned in the valley. No art can teach them; no rules of voice can make them perfectly sung. Their music is in the heart. They are songs of memory, of personal experience. They bring out their burden from the shadow of the past; they mount on the wings of yesterday.

St. John says that even in Heaven there will be a song that can only be fully sung by the sons of earth—the strain of redemption. Doubtless it is a song of triumph, a hymn of victory to the Christ who made us free. But the sense of triumph must come from the memory of the chain.

No angel, no archangel can sing it so sweetly as I can. To sing it as I sing it, they must pass through my exile, and this they cannot do. None can learn it but the children of the Cross.

And so, my soul, thou art receiving a music lesson from thy Father. Thou art being educated for the choir invisible. There are parts of the symphony that none can take but thee.

There are chords too minor for the angels. There may be heights in the symphony which are beyond the scale—heights which angels alone can reach; but there are depths which belong to *thee*, and can only be touched by thee.

George Matheson
1842–1906

150

BE HONEST WITH GOD

[A] way to encourage ourselves is to be honest with God. Don't try to hide your emotions from God. He can handle them. There is nothing He hasn't seen before or even experienced first-hand when He walked on earth. I'm a deep feeling person, and when I try to conceal my emotions from the Lord, it's like trying to hide an elephant in an open field. It took me many years of walking with God before I could believe that He wasn't going to punish me for my feelings.

Now, when I feel anger, I tell Him about it. God is even the object of my anger at times. No point in trying to hide it. Even if He couldn't read my thoughts He can see the frown creasing my brow as I pray. God has a lot to put up with in me. You know how some children get weepy when they are hurt and you want to cuddle them and hold them and kiss away the pain, and how others kick and scream and throw themselves on the floor and you want to send them to their rooms? That's me. I'm very reactive if I so much as stub my toe.

God doesn't wring His hands and break out in a sweat because I'm throwing myself around. Instead, He waits until I've worn myself out, then asks, "How can I help you?"

It doesn't work to deny our true emotions. Suppressing them only intensifies their power and delays the healing. It's as we become aware of our own pain and express it to God that He heals us.

Gloria Chisholm

THE POTENTIAL IN PERSONS

The wonderful thing about the Bible is that it does not take some Pollyanna view that everything is beautiful and that things will always turn out fine. Tragedy, suffering, and inhumanity do indeed exist, and no world view would be accurate if it did not take into account what Melville called the "blackness of things." All that notwithstanding, the Bible takes the view that men and women are God's good creation. Our self-centeredness often distorts that creation, but people have God-given dignity and goodness. "What is man that thou art mindful of him?" muses the psalmist. "Thou hast made him little less than God, and dost crown him with glory and honor."

Someone has said that one can look at the handicapped and ask, "How could God possibly allow blindness and deafness?" Or one can look at Helen Keller and see her great spirit, her great love, her great accomplishment. When she was given an honorary law degree at the University of Glasgow, she said in response, "It is a sign, Sir, that silence and darkness need not block progress of the immortal human spirit." And one is forced to say that there must be a great God in this world to produce such greatness.

Alan Loy McGinnis

I will give thee the treasures of darkness. (Isa. 45:3)

In the famous lace shops of Brussels, there are certain rooms devoted to the spinning of the finest and most delicate patterns. These rooms are altogether darkened, save for a light from one very small window, which falls directly upon the pattern. There is only one spinner in the room, and he sits where the narrow stream of light falls upon the threads of his weaving. "Thus," we are told by the guide, "do we secure our choicest products. Lace is always more delicately and beautifully woven when the worker himself is in the dark and only his pattern is in the light."

May it not be the same with us in our weaving? Sometimes it is very dark. We cannot understand what we are doing. We do not see the web we are weaving. We are not able to discover any beauty, and possible good in our experience. Yet if we are faithful and fail not *and faint not,* we shall some day know that the most exquisite work of all our life was done in those days when it was so dark.

If you are in the deep shadows because of some strange, mysterious providence, do not be afraid. Simply go on in faith and love, never doubting. God is watching, and He will bring good and beauty out of all your pain and tears.

J. R. Miller

God, make me brave for life: oh, braver than this.
Let me straighten after pain, as a tree straightens after the
    rain,
Shining and lovely again.
God, make me brave for life; much braver than this.
As the blown glass lifts, let me rise
From sorrow with quiet eyes,
Knowing Thy way is wise.
God, make me brave, life brings
Such blinding things.
Help me to keep my sight;
Help me to see aright
That out of dark comes light.

Author Unknown

THE CONQUEST OF LIMITATION

When a zealous, adventurous spirit is put in bonds, it may seem to be one of life's greatest tragedies. But when Paul was in prison, he wrote: "I hasten to assure you, brethren, that my circumstances here have only had the effect of spreading the Gospel further." A prison can be turned into a pulpit; all things cooperate unto good among those whose faith is in God. The major difference between human beings is not in what happens to them, but in how they react to what happens. Blindness makes some bitter; others, like Helen Keller, it makes apostles of inspiration. It is very easy for young men to see visions and to have the forward look in time; but to the old on whom the sun is casting a forward shadow, it is not easy to dream dreams. Time has no more illusions, or that perilous stuff from which dreams are compounded. Now the consoling

153

vision must be sought beyond time in the Timeless and beyond space in the Spaceless. Paul was never greater in his life
than when he saw stars through prison bars, and his heart
leaped in thankfulness for their distant light. Others looking
through the same bars see only mud.

Milton saw more through his blind eyes than men with
their seemingly seeing eyes, and therefore could write:

> I argue not
> Against Heaven's Hand or Will, nor bate a jot
> Of heart or hope, but still bear up and steer
> Right onward

Beethoven in his deafness heard melodies through other
ears than those which take in only noise.

Life is like a tapestry. We work from behind and with what
seems like meaningless little colored threads; but God sees the
finished pattern. In such assurance, Job cried out in his affliction: "I will trust Him though He slay me."

Bishop Fulton J. Sheen

A little boy passed a pet store every day on his way home
from school. Every day he would stop at that pet store and
play with the dozen or so puppies that were kept in a pen
in the display window. Finally he got up enough courage to
ask the owner of the pet shop how much one of the puppies
would cost. The owner of the shop told him the price, and the
boy went home and began saving his weekly allowance.

He returned a few weeks later with his piggy bank tucked
under his arm. Smiling broadly, he lifted his bank onto the
counter and broke it open. "It's all there!" he said joyfully.

"So I see!" said the owner, as he began to sort through the
nickels, dimes, and quarters on his counter. "There's the pen.
Pick out any puppy you like."

The puppies were yelping, wagging their tails, and crawling
all over each other—all but one who sat forlornly in one
corner of the pen. The boy reached past all the other puppies,

picking up the one lonely puppy in the corner. He brought it to the counter and presented it to the shop owner.

"Oh, you don't want that one," said the man.

"Why not?" asked the boy.

"Well, he's crippled. Just look at his leg. Son, you want a puppy who can run and play with you in the park. You don't want a crippled puppy."

The little boy set the puppy down on the floor and lifted the cuffs of his pants, revealing a set of braces, reminders of a crippling childhood disease of a few years before. "Yes, he's crippled. But I'm crippled too. I thought since we're both crippled, we could be better friends."

We're all crippled, aren't we?

Our wounds come in many different forms, but we're all crippled. We came to Christ to be healed, and in one bold, all-consuming stroke at the cross of Calvary we were healed of the crippling, terminal disease called *sin*. "By His wounds we are healed," says Isaiah 53:5.

Ron Lee Davis

The radiant Joni Eareckson Tada tells of a visit with Corrie ten Boom shortly before the elderly, brave Dutch woman died. Both were in wheelchairs—Joni having been paralyzed by a swimming accident, and Corrie having suffered a stroke:

That night in bed, I relive each moment of my visit with Corrie ten Boom. I recall how our eyes met as we were fed our cucumber sandwiches. Helpless and for the most part dependent, I felt our mutual weakness. Yet I am certain neither of us had ever felt stronger. It makes me think of the Cross of Christ—a symbol of weakness and humiliation, yet at the same time, a symbol of victory and strength. . . .

For a wheelchair may confine a body that is wasting away. But no wheelchair can confine the soul . . . the soul that is inwardly renewed day by day.

For paralyzed people can walk with the Lord.

Speechless people can talk with the Almighty.

Sightless people can see Jesus.
Deaf people can hear the Word of God.
And those like Tante Corrie, their minds shadowy and obscure, can have the very mind of Christ.

Joni Eareckson Tada

FOR ONE WHO IS TIRED

Dear Child,
God does not say today, "Be strong"—
  He knows your strength is spent—
He knows how long the road has been—
  How weary you've become, for
He who walked this earth alone—
  Each boggy lowland and each rugged hill,
    understands—
  And so He simply says, "Be still,
  Be still and know that I am God."
The hour is late and you must rest awhile,—
  And you must wait
Until life's empty reservoirs fill up
  As slow rain fills an empty unturned cup.
Hold up your cup, dear child, for God to fill.
  He only asks that you be still.

Grace Noll Crowell

HERE'S WHAT GOD WILL DO!

God offers *real* comfort. Not neurotic pity. Not a sympathy that only weakens the hurting person. He offers a tough love that turns us into sweeter and stronger persons!

When our daughter, Carol, lost her leg in a motorcycle accident at the age of thirteen, my wife and I fell over ourselves

156

trying to comfort her. We brought her favorite stuffed animals to the hospital, we called her friends and asked them to visit with her. We never left Carol's side; one of us was with her almost constantly.

Then one day we received a call from our friend, Dorothy DeBolt. As many of you know, Dorothy is the mother of fourteen adopted children. Those children are all very special. Some are blind, some are paraplegic. One is a quadruple amputee. All are physically or mentally challenged children.

Dorothy has done wonders with all of these children. Despite their handicaps, she has motivated them to do far more than anyone would ever have dreamed. They all dress themselves. There are no ramps in the house; they all know how to climb stairs so that they would never be barred anywhere by the absence of ramps.

When Dorothy heard about Carol's accident, she called to express her love and concern. Yes, she expressed *love* —she cared that Carol had experienced so much pain. And yes, she was *concerned*. She felt Arvella and I needed to be warned that there was a right way and a wrong way to help Carol.

She said simply, "Be careful how you comfort her."

How wise were her words. Carol needed comfort, not pity, and comfort came not by drying tears, but by lifting her attention beyond the present pain to the future victories.

God comforts. He doesn't pity. He doesn't commiserate. He picks us up, dries our tears, soothes our fears, and lifts our thoughts beyond the hurt.

How does God comfort us so masterfully? Five ways: (1) He gives us courage; (2) He gives us a sense of calm; (3) He gives us companionship; (4) He gives us compassion; and (5) He gives us a new set of commitments.

Robert Schuller

Hast thou not known?
Hast thou not heard,
　that the everlasting God,
　　the Lord,
　　　the Creator of the ends of the earth,

157

fainteth not,
     neither is weary?
there is no searching of His understanding.

He giveth power to the faint,
     and to them that have no might
     He increaseth strength.

Even the youths shall faint
     and be weary,
          and the young men shall utterly fall.

But they that wait upon the Lord
     shall renew their strength:
          they shall mount up with wings as eagles,
          they shall run and not be weary,
          and they shall walk,
               and not faint.

Isaiah 40:28–31

. . . I was as close to Jesus as I am to you when this thing happened. I don't suppose Lydia would have attempted it if she hadn't seen Jairus in the throng. That must have given her confidence. Summoning all her poor strength, she ran down the steps and into that crowd, desperately forced her way through, and struggled on until she was almost at Jesus' side. Then, her courage must have failed her; for, instead of trying to speak to him, she reached out and touched his Robe. I think she was frightened at her own audacity. She turned quickly and began forcing her way out.

'Why didn't some of you call Jesus' attention to her?' asked Marcellus.

'Well'—defended Justus—'there was a great deal of confusion—and it all happened so quickly—and then she was gone. But, instantly, Jesus stopped and turned about. "Who touched me?" he demanded.'

'You mean—he felt that contact—through his Robe?' exclaimed Marcellus.

Justus nodded—and went on.

'Simon and Philip reminded him that there were so many crowding about. Almost any of them might have brushed against him. But he wasn't satisfied with that. And while he stood there, questioning them, we heard this woman's shrill cry. They opened the way for her to come to him. It must have been a very trying moment for Lydia. She had lived such a sheltered life. The crowd grew suddenly quiet.'

Justus' voice was husky as he recovered the scene.

'I saw many pathetic sights, through those days,' he continued, 'but none more moving. Lydia came slowly, with her head bowed and her hands over her eyes. She knelt on the ground before Jesus and confessed that she was the one who had touched him. Then she lifted her eyes, with the tears running down her cheeks, and cried, "Master! I have been healed of my affliction!"'

Overcome by his emotions, Justus stopped to wipe his eyes on his sleeve. Steadying his voice with an effort, he went on:

'Everyone was deeply touched. The people were all in tears. Jairus was weeping like a child. Even Jesus, who was always well controlled, was so moved that his eyes were swimming as he looked down into Lydia's face. Marcellus—that woman gazed up at him as if she were staring into a blinding sunshine. Her body was shaking with sobs, but her face was enraptured! It was beautiful!'

'Please go on,' insisted Marcellus, when Justus fell silent.

'It was a very tender moment,' he said, thickly. 'Jesus gave her both of his hands and drew her gently to her feet; and then, as if he were speaking to a tearful little child,' he said, "Be comforted, my daughter, and go in peace. Your faith has made you whole."'

'That is the most beautiful story I ever heard, Justus,' said Marcellus, soberly.

'I hardly know why I told you,' muttered Justus. 'I've no reason to think you could believe that Lydia was cured of her malady merely by touching Jesus' Robe.'

He sat waiting, with an almost wistful interest, for a further comment from Marcellus. It was one thing to say of a narrative that it was a beautiful story; it was quite another thing to concede its veracity. Marcellus had been adept in contriving common-sense explanations of these Galilean mysteries. The story of Lydia's healing had obviously moved him, but doubtless he would come forward presently with an attempt to solve the problem on natural grounds. His anticipated argument was so long in coming that Justus searched his face intently, astonished at its gravity. He was still more astounded when Marcellus replied, in a tone of deep sincerity:

'Justus—I believe every word of it!'

Lloyd C. Douglas
(from *The Robe*)

THE WOMAN WHO CAME BEHIND HIM IN THE CROWD

Near him she stole, rank after rank;
    She feared approach too loud;
She touched his garment's hem, and shrank,
    Back in the sheltering crowd.

A shame-faced gladness thrills her frame:
    Her twelve years' fainting prayer
Is heard at last! she is the same
    As other women there!

She hears his voice. He looks about,
    Ah! is it kind or good
To drag her secret sorrow out
    Before that multitude?

The eyes of men she dares not meet—
    On her they straight must fall!
Forward she sped, and at his feet
    Fell down, and told him all.

To the one refuge she hath flown,
    The Godhead's burning flame!
Of all earth's women she alone
    Hears there the tenderest name!

"Daughter," he said, "be of good cheer;
  Thy faith hath made thee whole:"
With plenteous love, not healing mere,
  He comforteth her soul.

George Macdonald

Bless the Lord, O my soul:
  and all that is within me, bless his holy name.
Bless the Lord, O my soul,
  and forget not all his benefits:
Who forgiveth all thine iniquities;
  who healeth all thy diseases;
Who redeemeth thy life from destruction;
  who crowneth thee with loving-kindness and tender
    mercies;
Who satisfieth thy mouth with good things;
  so that thy youth is renewed like the eagle's.
The Lord executeth righteousness
  and judgment for all that are oppressed.
He made known his ways unto Moses,
  his acts unto the children of Israel.
The Lord is merciful and gracious,
  slow to anger, and plenteous in mercy.
He will not always chide:
  neither will he keep his anger for ever.
He hath not dealt with us after our sins;
  nor rewarded us according to our iniquities.
For as the heaven is high above the earth,
  so great is his mercy toward them that fear him.
As far as the east is from the west,
  so far hath he removed our transgressions from us.
Like as a father pitieth his children,
  so the Lord pitieth them that fear him.
For he knoweth our frame;
  he remembereth that we are dust.
As for man, his days are as grass:
  as a flower of the field, so he flourisheth.
For the wind passeth over it, and it is gone;
  and the place thereof shall know it no more.

But the mercy of the Lord is from everlasting to
    everlasting
upon them that fear him,
and his righteousness unto children's children;
To such as keep his covenant,
    and to those that remember his commandments to do
    them.
The Lord hath prepared his throne in the heavens;
    and his kingdom ruleth over all.

Psalm 103:1–19

As a gift he scatters the snow, which falls in flakes like
fleecy wool. Snow falls softly, covers universally and clothes
warmly, even as wool covers the sheep.

. . . It is wise to see God in winter and in distress as well
as in summer and prosperity. He who one day feeds us with
the finest of the wheat, at another time robes us in snow; he
is the same God in each case, and each form of his operation
bestows a gift on men.

Charles H. Spurgeon
1834–1892

ABOVE THE STORM

I remember being in a meeting after the Civil War had been
going on for about six months. The army of the North had
been defeated at Bull Run; in fact, we had nothing but defeat,
and it looked as though the Republic was going to pieces; so
we were much cast down and discouraged. At this meeting
every speaker for a while seemed as if he had hung his harp
upon the willow; it was one of the gloomiest meetings I ever
attended. Finally an old man with beautiful white hair got up
to speak, and his face literally shone.

"Young men," he said, "you do not talk like sons of the King.
Though it is dark just here, remember it is light somewhere
else." Then he went on to say that if it were dark all over the
world, it was light up around the Throne.

162

He told us he had come from the East, where a friend had described to him how he had been up a mountain to spend the night and see the sun rise. As the party were climbing up the mountain, and before they had reached the summit, a storm came on. This friend said to the guide:

"I will give this up; take me back."

The guide smiled, and replied: "I think we shall get above the storm soon."

On they went; and it was not long before they got up to where it was as calm as any summer evening. Down in the valley a terrible storm raged: they could hear the thunder rolling, and see the lightning's flash; but all was serene on the mountain top.

"And so, my young friends," continued the old man, "though all is dark around you, come a little higher, and the darkness will flee away."

Often when I have been inclined to get discouraged, I have thought of what he said. If you are down in the valley amidst the thick fog and the darkness, get a little higher; get nearer to Christ, and know more of Him.

D. L. Moody
1837–1899

TRIALS, TEARS, AND TRIUMPHS

I have drunk deeply of the cup of life. I have known days of darkness and of light, hours of tragedy and defeat and blessed moments in which it was all conquered at a wave of His hand and at the sound of His voice saying, as He said to Peter as He walked on the Sea of Galilee, "Be of good cheer; it is I, be not afraid" (Matthew 14:27).

I have heard no other voice with such power and authority and effect. I have found that it is He and He alone who can wipe the tears from my eyes and the grief from my heart and strengthen me to walk tall again in His light and service.

If there is a better way, please tell me. I have yet to discover it.

Trials, tears, and triumphs? I say of it all as Edwin Markham said it:

Defeat may serve as well as victory
To shake the soul and let the glory out.
When the great oak is straining in the wind,
The boughs drink in new beauty, and the trunk
Sends down a deeper root on the windward side.
Only the soul that knows the mighty grief
Can know the mighty rapture. Sorrows come
To stretch out spaces in the heart for joy.

This is not my hope. It is my experience—and I pray that it may be yours.

Dale Evans Rogers

Now our Lord Jesus Christ himself, and God, even our Father, which hath loved us, and hath given us everlasting consolation and good hope through grace, Comfort your hearts, and stablish you in every good word and work.

2 Thessalonians 2:16–17

There are times when skies are overcast, when spiritual things seem to have lost their meaning and God himself appears to be far away. This is where we are to do battle, to go on actively, and even aggressively, believing in the goodness and purpose of God; never mind what happens or what we feel.

Sometimes again we make progress, at other times we seem to do no more than maintain our footing. But the practised Christian soldier can at least do this. Paul says, "Even when you have fought to a standstill you may still stand your ground."

". . . . In my opinion whatever we may have to go through now is less than nothing compared with the magnificent future God has in store for us. The whole creation is on tiptoe to see the wonderful sight of the sons of God coming into their own. The world of creation cannot see as yet reality, not because it chooses to be blind, but because in God's purpose it has been so limited—yet it has been given hope. And the hope is that in the end the whole of created life will be rescued from the tyranny of change and decay, and have its share in that magnificent liberty which can only belong to the children of God!" [Rom. 8:18–23, PHILLIPS].

J. B. Phillips

ON THE TWENTY-THIRD PSALM

In "pastures green"? Not always; sometimes He
Who knoweth best, in kindness leadeth me
In weary ways, where heavy shadows be.

And by "still waters"? No, not always so;
Oft times the heavy tempest round me blow,
And o'er my soul the waves and billows go.

But when the storm beats loudest, and I cry
Aloud for help, the Master standeth by,
And whispers to my soul, "Lo, it is I."

So, where He leads me, I can safely go,
And in the blest hereafter I shall know,
Why, in His wisdom, He hath led me so.

Author Unknown

Grow old with me.
The best is yet to be.
The last of life
For which the first was made.
Our times are in His hands,
Who sayeth, "A whole I've planned."
Trust God. See all, nor be afraid.

Robert Browning
(From *Rabbi Ben Ezra*)

165

OUR TIMES ARE IN HIS HANDS

The implication in Robert Browning's poem is that God has a plan for the whole of our life, not just a part of it. The apostle Paul says it another way in Romans 12:1–2, "I appeal to you, therefore, brethren, by the mercies of God, to present your bodies as a living sacrifice, holy and acceptable to God, which is your spiritual worship. Do not be conformed to this world, but be transformed by the renewal of your mind, that you may prove what is the will of God, what is good and acceptable and perfect" (RSV).

God has a will and a purpose and a plan for every life. It's important for a person to pray about his goals, work diligently toward them and be tenacious in reaching them. Too many people give up too easily, especially in the athletic profession. Young men come to campus as athletes with lots of grandiose ideas about how great they will be and how many yards they will rush and how many tackles they will make and how they will go on to the pros and make millions of dollars. But these dreams often crumble into a shadowy memory because those who dream them don't have the tenacity to stick with their goals. So tenacity is a third technique toward having an abundant life.

When adversity strikes, when bad things happen, a person who lives the abundant life stays with his goals if they are deep within his heart and planned with God's direction.

Grant Teaff

RESPONSES

It is awesome to realize that at the end of our lives we will be the sum total of our responses to God's answers to our prayers, for God has chosen to be limited in His next action by our response to His previous answer.

The final outcome of our lives is decided by a life-long series of responses to God's answers to our prayers. The way we respond to God and then He, in turn, to us actually determines the direction our lives will take.

It would be wonderful if each response to God affected only our lives at that point and no more. But not so. One response triggers the domino principle that affects all the rest of life. A major wrong response slips or hurtles us into the path of lost opportunities and missed spiritual growth, limiting God from taking us down the path He intended and planned for us before the foundation of the world.

As I grow older, it is interesting to look back on what seemed to be my correct responses and wonder "what if" I had not followed God's leading in that initial word from Him. What if I had not obeyed His initial call of "behold, I set before you an open door" (Rev. 3:8), when I sought His face about the original prayer experiment that produced my prayer ministry? What path would I have taken? How far astray might I have gone before He would have given me another chance to respond correctly?

We really do determine our own spiritual growth rate, usefulness in God's program for the world, and new opportunities by the way we respond to Him. At any point, we can hinder or completely stop His divine plan for our lives by our rebellious or inadequate response to His answer. Only in eternity will we get a glimpse of "what might have been" had our responses not thwarted God's plan for us.

But with each step of obedience to God's answer to our prayers, He holds us gently yet firmly in that perfect path He has for us—walking hand in hand with Him. Obedience!

Evelyn Christenson

STAND STILL AND SEE

"I'm standing, Lord:
There is a mist that blinds my sight.
Steep jagged rocks, front, left and right,
Lower, dim, gigantic, in the night.
Where is the way?"

"I'm standing, Lord:—
Since Thou hast spoken, Lord, I see
Thou hast beset—these rocks are *Thee!*
And since Thy love encloses me,
I stand and sing."

Betty Stam

John and Betty Stam, aged twenty-seven and twenty-eight, were missionaries to China and were martyred by the Communists for their belief in Jesus Christ. (Their baby, Helen, was rescued by a Chinese Christian.) This account describes the spiritual triumph and peace they found through their Savior, even as they faced their executioners:

No one knows what passed between John and Betty, or what fears assailed those young hearts. Silence veils the hours sacred to Him alone who, for love of us, hung long hours in darkness upon a cross. Certain it is that He who is never nearer than when we need Him most sustained His children in that hour of trial. Betty was not overwhelmed, but was enabled to plan with all a mother's tenderness for the infant they might have to leave behind, alone and orphaned, amid such perils. Could that little life survive? And if it did, what then? But had they not given her to God in that so recent dedication service? Would not He care for His own?

Never was that little one more precious than when they looked their last on her baby sweetness, as they were roughly summoned the next morning and led out to die. Yet there was no weakening. Those who witnessed the tragedy marvelled, as they testify, at the calmness with which both John and Betty faced the worst their misguided enemies could do. Theirs was the moral, spiritual triumph, in that hour when the very forces of hell seemed to be let loose. Painfully bound with ropes, their hands behind them, stripped of their outer garments and John barefooted (he had given Betty his socks to wear) they passed down the street where he was known to many, while the Reds shouted their ridicule and called the people to come and see the execution.

Like their Master, they were led up a little hill outside the town. There, in a clump of pine trees, the Communists harangued the unwilling onlookers, too terror-stricken to utter protest—But no, one man broke the ranks! The doctor of the place and a Christian, he expressed the feelings of many when he fell on his knees and pleaded for the life of his friends. Angrily repulsed by the Reds, he still persisted, until he was dragged away as a prisoner, to suffer death when it appeared that he too was a follower of Christ.

John had turned to the leader of the band, asking mercy for this man, when he was sharply ordered to kneel—and the look of joy on his face, afterwards, told of the unseen Presence with them as his spirit was released. Betty was seen to quiver, but only for a moment. Bound as she was, she fell on her knees beside him. A quick command, the flash of a sword which mercifully she did not see—and they were reunited.

"Absent from the body . . . present with the Lord."

"Thanks be to God, which giveth us the victory through our Lord Jesus Christ."

"They shall walk with me in white; for they are worthy."

Mrs. Howard Taylor

NO COWARD SOUL IS MINE

No coward soul is mine,
No trembler in the world's storm-troubled sphere:
    I see Heaven's glories shine,
And faith shines equal, arming me from fear.

    O God within my breast,
Almighty, ever-present Deity!
    Life—that in me has rest,
As I—undying Life—have power in Thee.

    Vain are the thousand creeds
That move men's hearts: unutterably vain;

169

Worthless as wither'd weeds,
Or idlest froth amid the boundless main,

To waken doubt in one
Holding so fast by thine infinity;
So surely anchored on
The steadfast rock of immortality.

With wide-embracing love
Thy spirit animates eternal years,
Pervades and broods above,
Changes, sustains, dissolves, creates, and rears.

Though earth and man were gone,
And suns and universe ceased to be,
And Thou were left alone,
Every existence would exist in Thee.

There is not room for Death,
Nor atom that his might could render void:
Thou—THOU are Being and Breath,
And what Thou art may never be destroyed.

Emily Brontë
1818–1848

Jesus said unto her, I am the resurrection, and the life: he that believeth in me, though he were dead, yet shall he live: And whosoever liveth and believeth in me shall never die.

John 11:25–26

THE GLORY OF HIS RESURRECTION

If we are conformed to his image in his Incarnation and crucifixion, we shall also share the glory of his resurrection. "We shall also bear the image of the heavenly" (I Cor.

15:49). "We shall be like him, for we shall see him even as he is" (I John 3:2). If we contemplate the image of the glorified Christ, we shall be made like unto it, just as by contemplating the image of Christ crucified we are conformed to his death. We shall be drawn into his image, and identified with his form, and become a reflection of him. That reflection of his glory will shine forth in us even in this life, even as we share his agony and bear his cross. Our life will then be a progress from knowledge to knowledge, from glory to glory, to an ever closer conformity with the image of the Son of God. "But we all, with unveiled face reflecting as a mirror the glory of the Lord, are transformed into the same image from glory to glory" (II Cor. 3:18).

This is what we mean when we speak of Christ dwelling in our hearts. His life on earth is not finished yet, for he continues to live in the lives of his followers. Indeed it is wrong to speak of the Christian life: we should speak rather of Christ living in us. "I live, and yet no longer I, but Christ liveth in me" (Gal. 2:20). Jesus Christ, incarnate, crucified and glorified, has entered my life and taken charge. "To me to live is Christ" (Phil. 1:21).

Dietrich Bonhoeffer

Sandy Ford was a brilliant young scholar and athlete — a leader among his peers. But at twenty-one years of age he died of a rare heart disease. His father, Dr. Leighton Ford, returned to the track where Sandy had run so many races. Standing there at the starting line, he remembered:

Weeks after Sandy died, a letter came from the missionary under whose direction he worked that summer in France. He wrote, "We are so earthbound. We assume that the main part of God's will and work is here on earth. I believe that not only the best is yet to come, but the highest will also be there . . . *God never wastes anything* . . . rather than being the end, this is the Beginning!"

So I stand here on the track. With my toe, I draw a line where the finish line was, where Sandy finished his last race.

But the finish line is also the starting line. And that is what makes the pain bearable. That is what undergirds the loss with hope. That is what makes the race worth running. Suppose that life is not the race. Suppose life is only the training season, and Eternity is the real race.

Then Sandy's heart was beating, not just for a medley relay, not just twenty-one years, but for eternity. The weight he carried—including a wounded heart—was preparing him for an eternal weight of glory.

Sometimes in my mind, I whisper, "What is it like, son?"

And I hear him say, "I can think so deeply and every thought is clear. I can speak and express exactly what I mean. I can run and never get tired. I am so surefooted in the paths of glory."

So a son leaves a legacy for a father. I have determined to run my race for Christ to the end. And when that time comes maybe our Savior will let him come running to meet me. Then with all sons and daughters of the resurrection our hearts will beat and run for God forever.

Leighton Ford

EASTER DAY

In the Morning

O Lord Jesus Christ, who upon this day didst conquer death and rise from the dead, and who art alive for evermore, help us never to forget Thy Risen Presence for ever with us. Help us to remember,

That Thou are with us in every time of perplexity to guide and to direct;

That Thou art with us in every time of sorrow to comfort and to console;

That Thou art with us in every time of temptation to strengthen and to inspire;

That Thou art with us in every time of loneliness to cheer and to befriend;

That Thou art with us even in death to bring us through the waters to the glory on the other side.

Make us to be certain that there is nothing in time or eternity which can separate us from Thee, so that in Thy presence we may meet life with gallantry and death without fear.

This we ask for Thy love's sake.   AMEN.

In the Evening

O Lord Jesus Christ, forgive us for the times when we have forgotten Thy Risen Presence for ever with us.

Forgive us for times when we failed in some task, because we did not ask Thy help.

Forgive us for times when we fell to some temptation, because we tried to meet it by ourselves.

Forgive us for times when we were afraid, because we thought that we were alone in the dark.

Forgive us for times when we were driven to despair, because we were trying to fight the battle in our own unaided strength.

Forgive us for times when we said and did things which now we are ashamed to remember that Thou didst hear and Thou didst see.

Forgive us for times when death seemed very terrible, and the loss of loved ones beyond all bearing, because we forgot that Thou hadst conquered death.

Make us this night again to hear Thee say: Lo, I am with you always even unto the end of the world, and in that promise grant unto us to find courage and strength to meet all things undismayed.

This we ask for Thy love's sake.   AMEN.

William Barclay

Imagine the despair of Jesus' disciples! They had seen their beloved Lord die the most cruel and ignominious death. In almost uncontrollable grief they had gently taken Him down from the Cross and placed Him in a tomb carved out of rock. They had watched while a great boulder was rolled across the opening, with unrelenting finality. A finality that so many experience when they attend a loved one's funeral.

173

Fear and despair were their companions. All their hope was shattered—there was nothing for them to live for. The cause of Christianity was dead.

In the Apostles' Creed it says that He "was crucified, dead and buried." Could anything sound more final, more hopeless?

How beautiful are the following words, from the same Creed. "The third day He rose again from the dead; He ascended into heaven, and sitteth on the right hand of God the Father Almighty."

The knocking on the door and Mary Magdalene's urgent voice awakened the disciples out of their despair, as she told them that she had seen the Lord—that He had risen as He said He would! What joy, doubt, excitement must have crowded into their minds as they ran back to the garden, where the tomb was, and saw with their own eyes that the stone had been rolled away and that the tomb was empty! No gravestone would ever be inscribed HERE LIES JESUS CHRIST for he was *alive!*

What a difference this makes for you and me, for it means we never have to fear death—our Savior has conquered it. ". . . because I live, ye shall live also" (John 14:19). It means that through Him we shall know immortality and that when we stand at the graveside of a loved one it is *not* the end, for those who love Him. He has promised that He has gone on to prepare a place for us.

Christians all over the world will testify to the truth of Christ's Resurrection, for they sense His presence with them—the Living Risen Lord. It is the same Lord that walked in the cool of the garden that first Easter morning and spoke Mary's name. He speaks our names today, for He loves us and longs for our companionship too.

Each time we see the empty Cross let it remind us of the suffering of Jesus, but also the *victory.* In the words of Peter Marshall, "Let us never live another day as if *He* were dead!"

Joan Winmill Brown

So shall we ever be with the Lord. Wherefore comfort one another with these words.

1 Thessalonians 4:17–18

THE SOUL OF MAN

If the Father deigns to touch with divine power the cold and pulseless heart of the buried acorn and to make it burst forth from its prison walls, will He leave neglected in the earth the soul of man made in the image of his Creator?

William Jennings Bryan

ACCEPTING THE FUTURE

The Christian should never forget that he has a Friend Who stands by him, a Friend Who knows all about fear because He "set His face to go to Jerusalem," aware that the cross and death were waiting for Him there. The faith that this Risen Christ is beside him and that He is quite capable of controlling the future whatever evil may come, is a source of serenity and courage to many a humble Christian believer.

It is a paradox that the Christ Who died upon the cross should be able to bring such comfort to those who fear suffering and death, yet so it is. Professor Arnold Toynbee, the greatest living authority on world history . . . concluded his *magnum opus*, ten large volumes on the history of mankind. In these books he traces the rise and fall of civilisation after civilisation. He analyses the reasons why they rose and fell, the outside pressure, the internal corruption. Naturally we ask, will our civilisation also crash to destruction? Toynbee's answer is "Not necessarily. It depends on the religious response we make to the dangerous situation in which we find ourselves." He then describes a dream he had years ago—a dream which obviously made a deep spiritual impression upon him at the time and which has been a source of comfort and inspiration ever since. In his dream he pictured himself in Ampleforth Abbey in Yorkshire. Above the altar is suspended from the ceiling a huge cross. In his dream Professor Toynbee

175

saw himself clinging to the foot of the cross. He heard a voice saying, "Amplexus, expecta." (Cling and wait.) So Toynbee concludes his mighty study of history by giving this same message to mankind, afflicted as we are by all kinds of fears, "Cling to the cross and wait." The cross brings home to us the reality of the forgiving love of God and such "perfect love casteth out fear." Again the cross speaks to us of God's power to overcome—eventually—every kind of evil. In this faith let us learn the art of accepting the future.

Gordon Powell

Let not your heart be troubled: ye believe in God, believe also in me.

In my Father's house are many mansions: if it were not so, I would have told you. I go to prepare a place for you.

And if I go and prepare a place for you, I will come again, and receive you unto myself; that where I am, there ye may be also.

John 14:1–3

This One who walks like a king is named Jesus. They called Him the Nazarene or the Galilean. He called Himself the Son of man.

The common people speak of Him softly, with deep affection, such as the shepherds know, who carry the little lambs in their bosoms.

The beggars whisper His name in the streets as they pass, and the children may be heard singing about Him. His name has been breathed in prayer and whispered at night under the stars. He is known to the diseased, the human flotsam and jetsam that shuffles in and out of the towns and drifts hopelessly along the dusty highways of human misery.

His fame has trickled down to the streets of forgotten men, has seeped into the shadowed refuges of the unremembered women. It is Jesus of Nazareth.

Any outcast could tell you of Him. There are women whose lives have been changed who could tell you of Him—but not without tears. There are silent men—walking strangely as if unaccustomed to it—who speak of Him with lights in their eyes.

It is Jesus whom they are crowding to see. They want to look on His face to see the quality of His expression that seems to promise so much to the weary and the heavy-laden; that look that seems to offer healing of mind and soul and body;

forgiveness of sin;

another chance—a beginning again.

His look seemed to sing of tomorrow—a new tomorrow—

in which there should be no more pain

no more suffering

nor persecution

nor cruelty

nor hunger

nor neglect

nor disillusionments

nor broken promises

nor death.

Peter Marshall

THE HOPE OF HIS COMING

The promised coming of the Lord has been the great hope of true believers down through the centuries. Emil Brunner once said, "What oxygen is to the lungs, such is hope to the meaning of life." Some years ago in a Telstar discussion, Lord Montgomery asked General Eisenhower, "Can you give any hope?" Mr. Eisenhower prescribed a way out, "which if man misses," he said, "would lead to Armageddon." Winston Churchill's favorite American song was "The Battle Hymn of the Republic," which begins with the stirring phrase, "Mine eyes have seen the glory of the coming of the Lord."

The great creeds of the church teach that Christ is coming back. The Nicene Creed states that "He shall come again with glory to judge both the living and the dead." Charles Wesley wrote 7,000 hymns, and in 5,000 he mentioned the coming of Christ. When Queen Elizabeth II was crowned by the Archbishop of Canterbury, he laid the crown on her head with the sure pronouncement, "I give thee, O sovereign lady, this crown to wear until He who reserves the right to wear it shall return."

But till that time, one of America's best-known columnists summed it up when he said, "For us all, the world is disorderly and dangerous; ungoverned, and apparently ungovernable." The question arises: Who will restore order? Who can counter the danger of the nuclear holocaust? Who alone can govern the world? The answer is Jesus Christ!

Billy Graham

There is peace in heaven, peace purchased by the blood of his cross. There is peace in the hearts of his people who have come to that cross and experienced his salvation. But there will be no peace on earth until he returns and establishes his kingdom. "Of the increase of his government and peace there shall be no end, upon the throne of David, and upon his kingdom, to order it, and to establish it with judgment and with justice from henceforth even for ever. The zeal of the Lord of hosts will perform this" (Isaiah 9:7).

It is then that the great promises of peace found in the prophets will all be fulfilled. The lion will lie down with the lamb. The nations will beat their swords into plowshares. Men will study war no more.

Meanwhile, we wait for his coming. And as we wait, we enjoy his peace and we share his peace with a troubled world around us. We love him; we labor for him; we look for him. We long for that day when he shall reign, and when the breathtaking promises of Psalm 72 will be fulfilled: "The mountains shall bring peace to the people, and the little hills by righteousness. . . . He shall come down like rain upon the mown grass: as showers that water the earth. In his days shall the righteous flourish; and abundance of peace so long as the moon endureth" (verses 3, 6, 7).

Even so, come quickly, Lord Jesus!

Warren W. Wiersbe

The stars shine over the mountains,
   the stars shine over the sea,
The stars look up to the mighty God,
   the stars look down on me;
The stars shall last for a million years,
   a million years and a day,
But God and I will live and love
   when the stars have passed away.

Robert Louis Stevenson

⚞ Index of Authors and Sources ⚟

Scripture Index

Genesis
8:22 *25*
9:12–14 *25*
28:15 *142*

Judges
5:31 *51*

1 Samuel
16:7 *62*

1 Kings
8:56 *23*

Psalms
5:1–3 *50*
8 *53–54*
16:11 *95*
42:1–8 *101–102*
46 *131–132*
46:1–3 *149*
50:1 *96*
72:3,6,7 *178*
91 *143–144*
98:1–3 *112–113*
100 *86*
103:1–19
113:1–6 *51*
121 *134*
139:9–10 *123*
139:14 *41, 85*
139:17 *85*

Song of Solomon
8:6 *95*

Isaiah
9:7 *178*
35:7 *96*
40:28–31 *157–158*

45:3 *152*
53:3 *107*
53:5 *155*

Jeremiah
31:3 *13*
33:3 *29*

Malachi
4:2 *51*

Matthew
5:45,48 *26*
7:7–8 *29*
7:28–29 *58*
14:27 *148, 163*
18:10 *16*
22:39 *41*

Luke
7:37 *16*
19:9 *16*

John
11:25–26 *170*
13:17 *43*
14:1–3 *176*
14:19 *174*
14:21 *16*
15:11 *107*
15:13 *43*
16:33 *107*
20:19 *136*
21:17 *28*

Romans
8:18–23 *88, 165*
8:24 *145*
8:26–27 *127*
8:38–39 *144–145*

12:1–2 *166*
12:11 *67*

1 Corinthians
13:8 *25, 43*
15:49 *170–171*

2 Corinthians
3:18 *171*
9:8–9 *79*

Galatians
2:20 *171*

Philippians
1:21 *171*
4:6–7 *48, 113*

Colossians
1:20 *136*
3:16 *50*

1 Thessalonians
4:17–18 *174*

2 Thessalonians
2:16–17 *164*

Hebrews
12:2 *95*

James
1:19 *33*

1 Peter
1:8 *104*

1 John
3:2 *171*
3:16 *19*
4:9–10 *19*
4:21 *43*

‒‒✺ Acknowledgments ✺‒‒

Every effort has been made to trace the ownership of copyrighted material used in this book and to secure permission for its use. Should there be any inadvertent error or omission, the compiler and editor will be pleased to make the necessary corrections in future printings. Thanks are due to the following for permission to use copyrighted material:

Abingdon Press, for "Love's Motive," "Jesus' Love for Those He Taught," and "He Loved Life," from *The Life and Teachings of Jesus Christ* by Rev. Professor James S. Stewart, D.D. (first published 1933, also published by The Saint Andrew Press, Edinburgh), and for "A Person after God's Heart," from *Lord of the Impossible* by Lloyd John Ogilvie, copyright 1984.

Augsburg Publishing House, for "The Potential in Persons," from *Bringing Out the Best in People* by Alan Loy McGinnis, copyright © 1985 Augsburg Publishing House.

Anthony G. Bottagaro, for selection on pp. 36–37 from his book, *To Create a World More Human and More Divine.*

William Collins Sons & Co., Ltd., for "A Surrender of Self," from *Mere Christianity* by C. S. Lewis, copyright 1943, 1945 and 1952; for "Surprised by Joy," from *Surprised by Joy* by C. S. Lewis, copyright 1955; for "Easter Day," from *The Plain Man's Book of Prayer* by William Barclay, copyright 1959 by William Barclay.

Ron Lee Davis, for selection on pp. 154–155 from his book, *A Forgiving God in an Unforgiving World.* Copyright 1984 by Ron Lee Davis; published by Harvest House Publishers.

Doubleday & Company, for selection on pp. 20–21 from *Dear and Glorious Physician* by Taylor Caldwell, copyright 1959 by Reback and Reback; for "When the Winds Cry I Hear You" from *I've Got to Talk to Somebody, God* by Marjorie Holmes, copyright 1968, 1969 by Marjorie Holmes Mighell; for selection on pp. 37–38 from *Midstream* by Helen Keller, copyright 1929 by Helen Keller; and for "The Conquest of Limitation" from *Thoughts for Daily Living* by Fulton J. Sheen, Ph.D., D.D., copyright 1956 by Doubleday & Company, Inc.

Desmond Dunkerley, for poem by John Oxenham on p. 42, published in *Treasury of Joy and Enthusiasm* by Norman Vincent

187

on pp. 158–160 from *The Robe* by Lloyd C. Douglas, copyright 1942 by Lloyd C. Douglas, copyright renewed 1969 by Virginia Douglas Dawson and Betty Douglas Wilson.

InterVarsity Press, for "God's Gift of Peace," from *Knowing God* by J. I. Packer, copyright 1973 by J. I. Packer.

Twila Knaack for selection on pp. 95–96 from her book, *Special Friends* by Twila Knaack, published by Word, Inc. in 1981.

Alfred A. Knopf, Inc., for selection on pp. 61–62 from *Markings* by Dag Hammarskjöld. Translated by Leif Sjoberg & W. H. Auden. Translation copyright 1964 by Alfred A. Knopf, Inc. and Faber & Faber Ltd.

McGraw-Hill Book Company, for "The Need for God," from *Adventures in Two Worlds* by A. J. Cronin. Copyright 1952 by McGraw-Hill Book Company.

Macmillan Publishing Company, for selection on pp. 100–101 from *Your God Is Too Small* by J. B. Phillips, copyright © J. B. Phillips, 1953; for selection on pp. 164–165 from *Good News: Thoughts on God and Man* by J. B. Phillips, copyright © J. B. Phillips, 1963; for "The Glory of His Resurrection," from *The Cost of Discipleship* by Dietrich Bonhoeffer, copyright 1963; and for "Love," from *Ethics*, by Dietrich Bonhoeffer, copyright 1965.

Wm. Morrow and Company, Inc., for selection on p. 142 from *The Shoes of the Fisherman* by Morris L. West. Copyright 1963 by Morris L. West.

Thomas Nelson, Inc., for selection by Jill Briscoe on pp. 25–26 from *Songs from Heaven and Earth* by Jill and Stuart Briscoe. Copyright 1985 by Thomas Nelson, Inc.

Harold Ober Associates, Incorporated, for selection on p. 148 from *The Bird in the Tree* by Elizabeth Goudge, copyright © 1940 by Elizabeth Goudge; and for "The Gift of Faith," from *A Book of Faith* by Elizabeth Goudge, copyright © 1976 by Elizabeth Goudge.

Overseas Missionary Fellowship (formerly China Inland Mission) for selection on p. 113 by Hudson Taylor; for "Seeming Defeat," from *In the Arena* by Isobel Kuhn, copyright 1959 China Inland Mission; for "Stand Still and See," by Betty Stam and the selection on pp. 168–169 by Mrs. Howard Taylor, both from *The Triumph of John and Betty Stam* by Mrs. Howard Taylor, copyright 1935 China Inland Mission.

Pantheon Books, a Division of Random House, Inc., for selection on p. 55 from *Gift from the Sea* by Anne Morrow Lindbergh. Copyright © 1955 by Anne Morrow Lindbergh.

Paulist Press, for selection on pp. 86–87 from *That Man Is You* by
Louis Evely, translated by Edmond Bonin. Copyright 1964 by The
Missionary Society of St. Paul the Apostle in the State of New
York.

Eugenia Price, for "Broken Alabaster and a Mended Heart" from
Beloved World: The Story of God and People by Eugenia Price.
Published 1971 by The Zondervan Corporation.

Fleming H. Revell Company, for selection on pp. 16–17 from *The
Christian's Secret of a Happy Life* by Hannah Whitall Smith, para-
phrased by Catherine Jackson, copyright © 1979 by Catherine
Jackson; for "We're Loved," from *God's Promises for You* by Roger
Palms, copyright © 1977 by Roger Palms; for selection on
pp. 42–43 from *Treasury of Joy and Enthusiasm* by Norman Vincent
Peale, copyright © 1981 by Norman Vincent Peale; for "Worry
and Worship," from *It's My Turn* by Ruth Bell Graham, copyright
© 1982 by Ruth Bell Graham; for selection on p. 50 from *A Closer
Walk* by Catherine Marshall, copyright © 1986 by Leonard
LeSourd, published by Chosen Books, Fleming H. Revell Company; for selection on pp. 52–53 from *Heaven Can't Wait* by Peter
Marshall, copyright © 1963 by Catherine Marshall, published by
Chosen Books, Fleming H. Revell Company; for selection on pp.
75–76 from *Mr. Jones, Meet the Master* by Peter Marshall, copyright © 1949, 1950 by Fleming H. Revell Company and renewed
1977, 1978 by Catherine Marshall LeSourd; for "Lord, Make Me
Generous," from *A Deeper Joy* by Colleen Townsend Evans, copyright © 1982 by Colleen Townsend Evans; for "Hallowed Be Thy
Name," from *Victorious Praying* by Alan Redpath, copyright ©
1957 by Fleming H. Revell Company and renewed 1985 by Alan
Redpath; for "God's Divine Lessons," from *Tramp for the Lord* by
Corrie ten Boom with Jamie Buckingham, copyright © 1974
by Corrie ten Boom and Jamie Buckingham; for selection on p. 96
from *Whispers of His Power* by Amy Carmichael, copyright © 1982
by the Dohnaver Fellowship; for selection on pp. 104–105 from
The Double Win by Denis E. Waitley, copyright © 1985 by Denis E.
Waitley; for selection on pp. 107–108 from *The Miracle of the Holy
Spirit* by Charles L. Allen, copyright © 1974 by Fleming H. Revell
Company; for selection on p. 111 from *Victorious Christian Living*
by Alan Redpath, copyright © 1955 by Fleming H. Revell Com-
pany and renewed 1983 by Alan Redpath; for "Remembering
Corrie ten Boom's Family," from *Corrie: The Lives She's Touched* by
Joan Winmill Brown, copyright © 1979 by Joan Winmill Brown;

for selection on pp. 138–140 from *Something More* by Catherine Marshall, copyright © 1974 by Catherine Marshall; for selection on pp. 148–149 from *A Way of Seeing* by Edith Schaeffer, copyright © 1977 by Edith Schaeffer; for selection on pp. 163–164 from *Trials, Tears and Triumphs* by Dale Evans Rogers, copyright © 1977 by Fleming H. Revell Company; for selection on pp. 173–174 from *Every Knee Shall Bow* by Joan Winmill Brown, copyright © 1978 by Joan Winmill Brown.

Roth Publishing, Inc. for "Alchemy," by Francis Carlin, published in *Anthology of Catholic Poets*, edited by Joyce Kilmer, first published by Halycon House, 1940.

The Saint Andrew Press, for "Love's Motive," "Jesus' Love for Those He Taught," and "He Loved Life," from *Life and Teachings of Jesus Christ* by The Rev. Professor James S. Stewart, D.D. (first edition published 1933; published in U. S. by Abingdon Press).

Harold Shaw Publishers, Box 567, Wheaton, IL 60189, for selection on pp. 128–129 from *Walking on Water: Reflections on Faith and Art* by Madeleine L'Engle, copyright © Crosswicks Ltd., 1980; for selection on pp. 164–165 from *The Price of Success* by J. B. Phillips, copyright © 1984, J. B. Phillips.

Tyndale House Publishers, Inc. for selection on p. 178 from *His Name Is Wonderful* by Warren W. Wiersbe, published by Tyndale House Publishers, Inc., © 1976.

Word, Inc., for "What Is God Like?" from *Peace With God* by Billy Graham, copyright 1953, 1984 by Billy Graham; for "Jesus Answers Our Need for Love," from *It's Friday, But Sunday's Comin'* by Anthony Campolo, copyright 1984 by Anthony Campolo; for "The Magnificence of God's Love" and "The Christian and Anxiety," from *Tough Truths for Today's Living* by D. Stuart Briscoe, copyright 1978 by Word, Inc.; for "The Quintessence of God's Love" and "Be Honest with God," from *Encourage One Another* by Gloria Chisholm, copyright 1986 by Gloria Chisholm; for "When God Says No," from *The ACTS of Joanna* by Anne Ortlund, copyright 1982 by Word, Inc.; for "Healing a Broken World," from *Salt for Society* by W. Phillip Keller, copyright 1981 by W. Phillip Keller; for selection on p. 38 from *Strengthening Your Grip* by Charles R. Swindoll, copyright 1982 by Charles R. Swindoll; for "A New Church for a New Day," from *No Longer Strangers* by Bruce Larson, copyright 1971, 1985 by Word, Inc.; for selection on pp. 41–42 from *Plan to Win* by Bill Glass and James E. McEachern, copyright 1984 by Word, Inc.; for selection on pp.